HARVEY

DEVASTATION, COURAGE, and RECOVERY in the EYE OF THE STORM

★ **THE TEXAS TRIBUNE**

TRIUMPH
BOOKS

This book is available in quantity at special discounts for your group or organization. For further information, contact:

Triumph Books LLC
814 North Franklin Street
Chicago, Illinois 60610
(312) 337-0747
www.triumphbooks.com

Printed in U.S.A.
ISBN: 978-1-62937-585-4
Design by Patricia Frey

The Texas Tribune is a nonprofit, nonpartisan public service news organization that educates and engages Texans on matters of Texas politics, policy and government through free news, data and events. Visit our website at www.texastribune.org.

With a presence in every ZIP code in America, The Salvation Army serves survivors before, during and after disasters, for however long it takes. In the aftermath of Hurricane Harvey, they will continue to provide physical, emotional and spiritual support to communities as they rebuild.

Michael Stravato

CONTENTS

INTRODUCTION

When your state is smacked head-on by a hurricane, when coastal communities are nearly wiped off the map, when the fourth-largest city in America is submerged in floodwater, a public-service newsroom doesn't think twice. It springs into action.

That's what happened at The Texas Tribune when Hurricane Harvey made landfall in Texas.

It was a storm scenario our reporters had anxiously and repeatedly warned of in the last year with colleagues at ProPublica and Reveal from the Center for Investigative Reporting:

Harvey's powerful winds — a Category 4 upon impact near Rockport, the strongest Texas hurricane in half a century — demolished beachfront communities, wrecking vacation homes and trailer parks alike, and tossing boats and cars around like confetti.

And its unprecedented rainfall — a mind-boggling 52 inches — drowned Houston, an already flood-prone city of more than 2 million, as well as communities up and down the coast. Highways turned into wave pools, full neighborhoods into lakes. Bayous breached their borders and reservoirs spilled into streets.

Locals, many of whom heeded officials' calls to shelter in place, were forced to make daring escapes as the floodwaters rose, or await brave first responders, many of them good Samaritans who hurtled into the storm in airboats, canoes or monster trucks.

Sadly, not everyone made it to safety.

An elderly couple and their four great-grandchildren died when floodwaters swept their van off of the road.

A woman drowned in a rain-swollen canal while trying to carry her toddler to safety; the three-year-old, who survived, was found clinging to her mother.

Four volunteer rescuers perished when a strong current dragged their boat into a power line.

A 34-year veteran of the Houston Police Department drowned in his car trying to get back to work.

Amid these chilling tales and heartbreaking losses came the devastating tallies: More than 80 deaths. An estimated $180 billion in damage. Enough debris to fill a college football stadium more than 100 times over. And thousands of coastal residents with nowhere to live, nowhere to attend school, no semblance of normalcy in their futures. At the height of the storm, 30,000 Texans turned to emergency shelters.

And there were questions: about warnings that went unheeded, about Houston's lax development policies, about flooded

Buffalo Bayou jumped its banks and flooded downtown Houston on Sunday, Aug. 27, 2017. Photo by Michael Stravato

neighborhoods that had rebuilt time and again, about the paving over of wetlands that would've provided an environmental buffer.

But more than anything else, there were selfless acts of heroism, from the first responders who evacuated their own families before heading back into chest-deep water, to the "Cajun Navy" — out-of-state volunteers who piloted their personal boats on around-the-clock rescue missions.

Hurricane Harvey amplified the strength, resilience and heart of the state's coastal region. It showcased the unbelievable generosity of fellow Texans, who opened up their homes and their wallets to countless evacuees. And it highlighted just how well the state's leaders could work together when they put deep partisan divisions aside.

This natural disaster also underscored The Texas Tribune's role as a trusted and reliable source of information at home and around the globe, giving our newsroom a sense of responsibility like never before. We owe a debt of gratitude to our national investigative reporting partners, ProPublica and Reveal.

In a *New York Times* op-ed published Aug. 30, columnist David Leonhardt wrote in "Houston, Warned" of our prescient investigative reporting projects of the last year, which foretold how Houston was ripe for the perfect storm.

When the national spotlight moves away, The Texas Tribune and its partners ProPublica and Reveal will still be on the ground in Houston, devoting real resources to asking the tough questions that are crucial to this battered region's future. ⭐

—Emily Ramshaw, Texas Tribune Editor-in-Chief

The Theater District in downtown Houston is flooded by water from Buffalo Bayou after it jumped its banks on Sunday, Aug. 22, 2017. Photo by Michael Stravato

AVENIDA HOUSTON WELCOME T

7'0" CLEARANCE

PART 1
BEFORE
THE STORM

WHY HOUSTON **ISN'T READY** FOR **HURRICANE HARVEY**

Last year, The Texas Tribune, ProPublica and Reveal from the Center for Investigative Reporting investigated Houston's vulnerability to hurricanes and torrential rainstorms. The nation's fourth-largest city is sure to see the latter in the coming days. Here's what we know about what could happen.

By Neena Satija, Kiah Collier and Al Shaw | August 25, 2017

The brunt of Hurricane Harvey is projected to miss Houston, but the sprawling metropolis is likely to face massive flooding from its third crippling storm in the past three years.

It underscores a new reality for the nation's fourth-largest city: Climate change is making such storms more routine. Meanwhile, unchecked development in the Houston area is wiping out the pasture land that once soaked up floodwaters. Last year, we explored in detail how Houston's rapid expansion has greatly worsened the danger posed by flooding.

How bad things get in Houston depends on where and how quickly the rain falls. But many are already drawing comparisons to 2001's Tropical Storm Allison — the worst rainstorm to hit an American city in modern history. Allison dropped 40 inches of rain on the city in five days, killed nearly two dozen people and caused $5 billion in damage in the county that includes Houston. The map on the next page shows how many homes, businesses, schools and other structures flooded. As you can see, a lot of flooded areas were outside the 100-year floodplain — the area the federal government says faces a 1 percent chance of flooding every year.

Tropical Storm Allison largely spared western parts of the Houston area. But that wasn't the case during a more recent storm that also crippled the sprawling metropolis. A flood in April 2016 — nicknamed the "Tax Day" flood because it fell on the deadline to file federal income taxes — paralyzed northwestern portions of the city and surrounding suburbs. Those areas have exploded in population in recent years.

Interstate 45 in downtown Houston on Sunday, Aug. 27, 2017 after heavy rains from Harvey. Photo by Michael Stravato

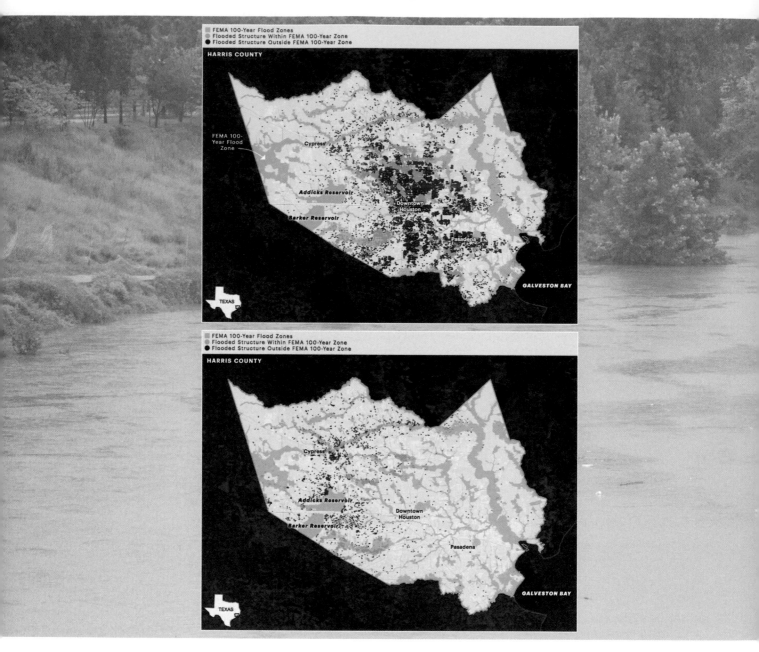

The Tax Day flood happened just 11 months after another devastating event — the "Memorial Day" flood in May 2015, which swept through areas north and west of downtown Houston. Again, many neighborhoods outside the known floodplain ended up underwater.

Together, the Memorial and Tax Day floods killed 16 people and caused well over $1 billion in property damage. Such torrential rains are supposed to be a rarity, but Houston's history is punctuated by major back-to-back storms.

Many residents say they are becoming more frequent and severe, and scientists agree.

"More people die here than anywhere else from floods," Sam Brody, a Texas A&M University at Galveston researcher, told us last year. "More property per capita is lost here. And the problem's getting worse."

Why?

Many scientists, experts and federal officials say Houston's explosive growth is largely to blame, along with climate change. As millions have flocked to the metropolitan area in recent decades, local officials have largely

rejected stricter building regulations, allowing developers to pave over acres of prairie land that once absorbed large amounts of rainwater. In the decade after Tropical Storm Allison, about 167,000 acres were developed in Harris County, home to Houston. The map above shows that a lot of the new development is in or near floodplains.

Some local officials flat-out disagree with the scientific evidence that shows development has worsened the effects of big storms. Mike Talbott, the former longtime head of the local flood control agency, told The Texas Tribune

and ProPublica last year that large-scale public works projects — like drainage basins — are reversing all the effects of Houston's recent growth (his successor shares that view).

"You need to find some better experts," Talbott said. When asked for names, he would only say, "starting here, with me." ★

Neena Satija reports for both The Texas Tribune and Reveal. Al Shaw reports for ProPublica.

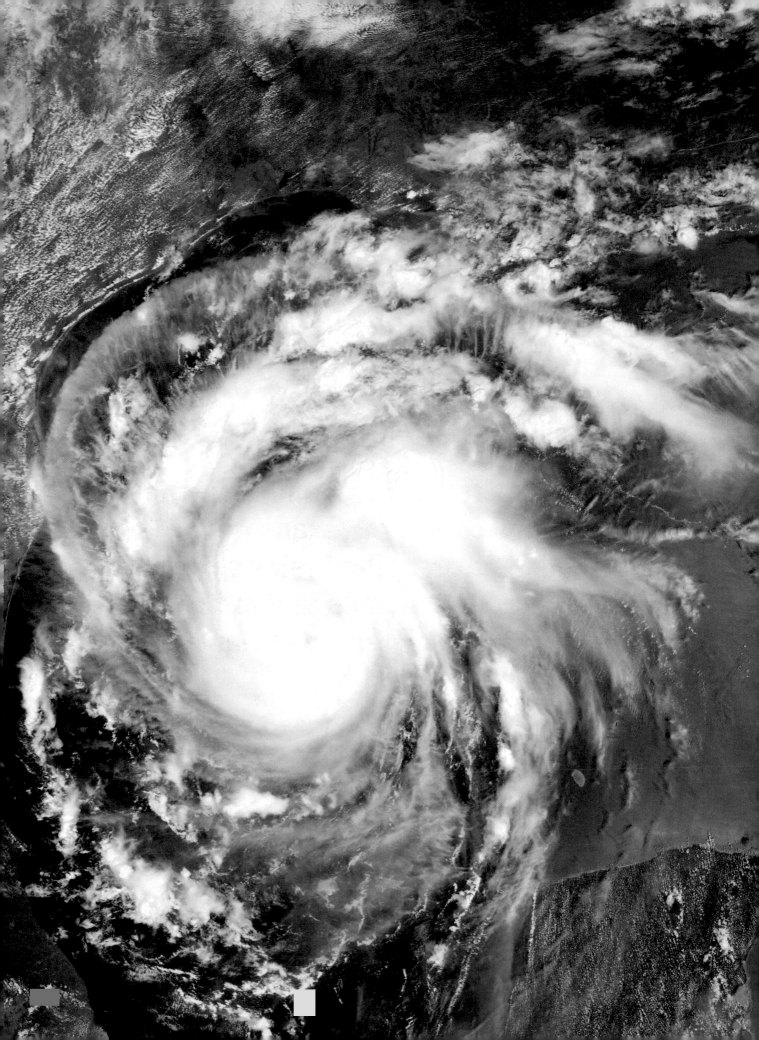

AS HARVEY DRAWS NEARER, SOUTH TEXANS HEAD NORTH

Amid warnings from family and memories of past hurricanes, scores of Texans in the Corpus Christi area are grabbing their belongings, boarding up their homes and hitting the highway to flee Hurricane Harvey.

By Brandon Formby | August 25, 2017

LIVE OAK COUNTY – Victor Lara rattles off with great ease the roster of hurricanes and tropical storms that have threatened or directly hit the Texas Coast in the past six decades. No matter how menacing they seemed as they moved up the gulf, the Corpus Christi resident always stayed at home and waited them out.

Harvey won't be getting that same reception.

Early Friday morning, Lara and his wife, Mary Lou Isaguirre, stood outside an Exxon gas station about 80 miles north of home and said they planned to let this weekend's expected disaster play out without them. The couple had hours earlier boarded up their house on Corpus Christi's southside, grabbed as many belongings as they could and begun the trek to a hotel more than 400 miles away in Fort Stockton.

This satellite image provided by NASA on Thursday, Aug. 24, 2017 shows Hurricane Harvey off the Gulf of Mexico. Harvey intensified as it steered toward the Texas coast on Friday, with forecasters saying it had strengthened to a Category 2 storm with the potential to swamp communities more than 100 miles (161 kilometers) inland. (NASA via AP)

15

"They said it's gonna be stationary, it's not going to move, it's going to dump a lot of rain," Lara said, of the looming hurricane, before he and his wife continued north again on Interstate 37.

Harvey is expected to be a Category 3 hurricane with wind gusts more than 110 miles per hour when it makes landfall late Friday or early Saturday. The wind speeds, storm surge and flooding from rainfall are expected to pose high to extreme risks to people and property across a wide swath of southern Texas, according to the National Weather Service. Rainfall east of Interstate 37 is expected to be between 15 and 25 inches, with the storm pouring as much as 35 inches on some areas.

Houston has already experienced deadly floods in recent years that caused more than $1 billion worth of damage. The Texas Tribune and ProPublica last year found that the state's biggest city is largely unprepared for a major hurricane.

President Donald Trump offered Texas federal support on Thursday. Gov. Greg Abbott has already declared a state of disaster for 30 Texas counties. Officials in several counties have issued mandatory evacuations. Corpus Christi and Galveston officials have issued voluntary evacuations.

It's the forecasts of dozens of inches of rain – and subsequent flooding – that prompted Lara to evacuate his home for the first time in his life.

Lara recalled not even evacuating for Celia back in 1970, which hit Texas' middle coast as a Category 3. A storm that reached Category 3 or higher is classified as a major hurricane.

A boarded up home in Rockport on Aug. 28, 2017, three days after Hurricane Harvey made landfall. Photo by Bob Daemmrich

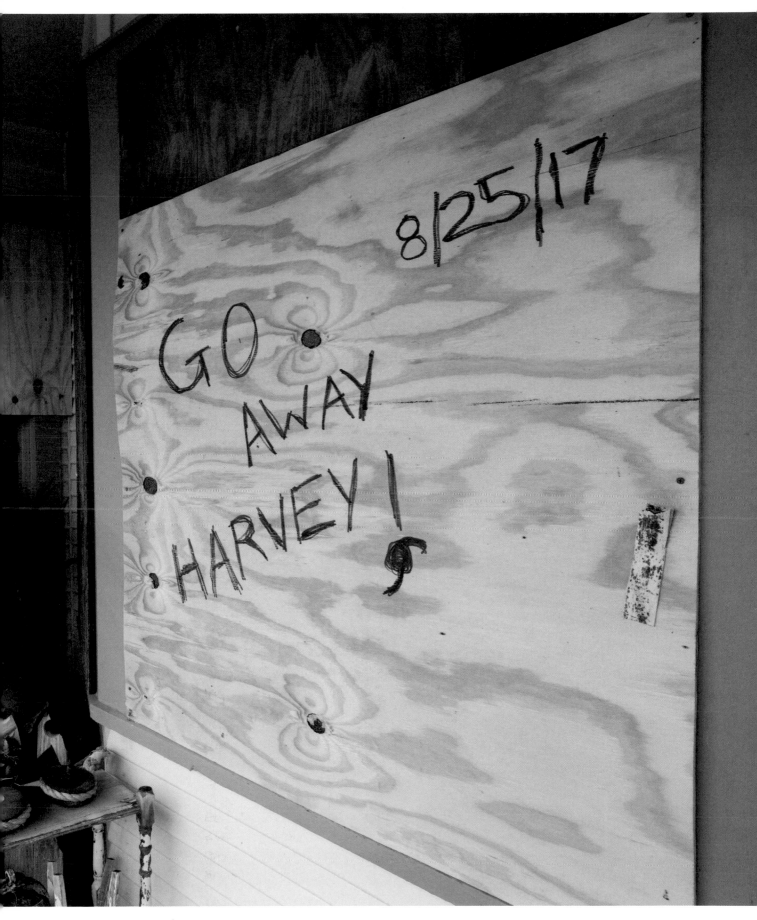

Celia hit Corpus Christi dead on and devastated the house next door to Lara's family.

"His whole roof fell in my backyard," Lara said. "But our house wasn't even damaged."

Like Celia, Harvey is expected to reach Texas as a Category 3.

If evacuation orders continue — and more Texans like Lara and Isaguirre voluntarily leave — southern Texas highways are expected to become log-jammed.

"That's why we left tonight, because my mom said she did not want to be sitting through traffic," said Melody Guerrero, whose family also stopped at the same gas station as Lara and Isaguirre. "Plus we know it's going to start raining."

Guerrero's father didn't want to leave their Corpus Christi home, but his wife and kids talked him into it after they started receiving phone calls from relatives all over the globe.

"We were freaked out enough to leave," Luis Guerrero said as he pumped gas into one of the family's three cars. "We're not going to risk anything."

Even loved ones in Houston called to ask if the family was safe. Alex Guerrero, one of Luis Guerrero's two sons, said he knew those relatives may not fathom Harvey's potential impact when they offered the family a place to stay.

"We were like, 'Nope,'" Alex Guerrero said before getting back in his car and joining his family's caravan to San Antonio. ⭐

Officials at the State of Texas Emergency Command Center at Department of Public Safety headquarters in Austin, Texas monitor Hurricane Harvey Saturday morning, Aug. 26, 2017. (Ralph Barrera/Austin American-Statesman via AP)

OFFICIALS SEND TEXANS MIXED MESSAGES ON EVACUATIONS

In the hours before Hurricane Harvey hits Texas, some local leaders told residents to flee their homes, while others urged them to stay in place and wait out the storm.

By Brandon Formby and Edgar Walters | August 25, 2017

CORPUS CHRISTI — Hurricane Harvey will reach Texas land overnight, but that is likely to be just the beginning of the powerful storm's wrath.

Some southern Texans were told to stay in place. Others were ordered to evacuate. All were warned to prepare for catastrophic flooding and power outages that could last up to seven days.

As winds whipped the nearby beach in this coastal city Friday morning, Kevin Murphy and two friends were virtually alone on the city streets as they boarded up the salon he owns.

"It floods downtown easily," Gary Acuna said after he used a power drill to screw in boards over the windows of Tease Salon.

Nueces County officials soon after told residents that they'd missed their window to leave and warned them to stay indoors and wait out the storm. Because Harvey is expected to linger over southern Texas, wind and rain are expected to wreak havoc for days.

"This storm is not going to play out overnight," Nueces County Judge Loyd Neal said at a Friday afternoon news conference.

He said people could be without power for days.

"Fry those weiners today and eat them for three days," he said.

Residents in Corpus Christi and the rest of Nueces County were not given mandatory evacuation orders, though those living in low-lying areas were encouraged to leave. But people living in several cities and counties farther east along the coast had already been ordered

Foster Adams, left, walks his dog, Gus, with his friend Bradley Strayer along the seawall during Hurricane Harvey in Corpus Christi, Texas, on Friday, Aug. 25, 2017. Hurricane Harvey is expected to make landfall on the Texas coast Friday night or early Saturday morning. (Nick Wagner/ Austin American-Statesman via AP)

to leave by Friday evening. That included a large swath of the state where Harvey is expected to reach land. Because so many Texans in the mid-coastal region were expected to be fleeing the storm, officials on the eastern coast urged their residents to remain in place to prevent nightmarish logjams on state highways.

Houston Mayor Sylvester Turner told people living in the state's largest city not to leave, citing "chaotic" traffic from the 2005 evacuations ahead of Hurricane Rita.

"Please think twice before trying to leave Houston en masse," Turner said through Twitter Friday afternoon. "No evacuation orders have been issued."

His city is among those expected to be inundated with rain for days. Houston is already infamous for being home to deadly floods in recent years and is not prepared for a major hurricane, The Texas Tribune and ProPublica reported last year.

Turner's advice contradicted that of Gov. Greg Abbott.

Asked at a news conference in Austin if he could put pressure on local leaders to encourage more evacuations, the governor said: "I can be suggestive of what I would do, and that is, if I were living in the Houston region, as I once did, I would decide to head to areas north of there."

Still, Abbott stressed that whether to call for mandatory evacuations was a decision best left to local leaders, who he said can make better judgments for their areas.

"I would urge everybody who has the possibility to consider evacuating as soon as possible," the governor said.

Water is flying off the shelves at a supermarket in Houston on Friday, Aug. 25, 2017. Photo by Michael Stravato

The governor briefed reporters after a statewide emergency preparedness call with Texas officials. The state has 41,000 shelter beds available for evacuees and more than 200 buses available to transport Texans out of coastal areas such as Corpus Christi, where storm surge and flooding are expected to pose the greatest risks. Texas state parks are also available for evacuees to stay at no cost.

"We are going to be dealing with immense, really record-setting flooding," Abbott said.

Corpus Christi Mayor Joe McComb defended the decision to stop short of making the evacuation order in his city mandatory. At a news conference, McComb said officials had a lot of discussion about the matter. He said he was "just the messenger," then immediately conceded that the decision was up to him and Neal, the county judge. He said the decision was made "based on the information we were given."

"And I think time will prove us right," he said. "I hope it does."

Murphy, the salon owner, said he plans to wait out the storm this weekend with the friends who helped him board up his business earlier in the day. They have plenty of food and a power generator.

"Very little water, but we got plenty of alcohol," Murphy's friend Acuna said.

But, of course, there is some anxiety about what the next several days will bring.

"Maybe a little," Murphy said with a sheepish smile from the passenger seat of a pickup truck outside his salon. ★

Evacuees watch a weather report inside the George R. Brown Convention Center in Houston on Sunday, Aug. 27, 2017. Photo by Michael Stravato

Hundreds of evacuees from flooded areas of Houston arrive at a Red Cross shelter set up at the George R. Brown Convention Center in downtown Houston on Sunday, Aug. 27, 2017. Photo by Michael Stravato

NO FIREARMS OR
WEAPONS OF
ANYKIND
ALLOWED INSIDE

PART 2
HARVEY HITS HOUSTON

HURRICANE HARVEY SLAMS TEXAS

The storm wreaked havoc on buildings along the Texas coast and continued to dump heavy rainfall on the region, prompting concerns of possibly disastrous flooding, while widespread power outages hampered the state's relief efforts.

By Edgar Walters and Shannon Najmabadi | August 26, 2017

At least one person has died since Hurricane Harvey slammed into the Texas coast near Rockport and Port Aransas, local officials said Saturday.

Aransas County Judge C.H. "Burt" Mills Jr. said at a news conference that one person in the county was killed after being caught in a fire in their home during the storm. Mills, who grew emotional as he spoke, said his community was nonetheless staying strong and that it was shocking to see the damage brought by the storm.

"When you see some buildings that you thought were going to be here forever – and some of them have been here forever – gone, it's shocking," Mills said. He said 12 to 14 people also suffered minor injuries.

Aransas County Sheriff Bill Mills told the Corpus Christi Caller-Times 30 to 40 others remained unaccounted for as of Saturday night.

Rescue boats fill a flooded street as people are evacuated after Tropical Storm Harvey on Monday, Aug. 28, 2017, in Houston. (AP Photo/David J. Phillip)

Harvey moved farther inland since coming ashore late Friday night, and by Saturday afternoon it had been downgraded to a tropical storm. But it's already wreaked havoc on buildings along the Texas coast, and it is expected to hover over the state's southern coastline and dump heavy rain for days — prompting concerns of possibly disastrous flooding.

Meanwhile, Gov. Greg Abbott and top emergency officials announced Saturday that the state's search-and-rescue operations had begun in earnest.

Speaking to reporters in the state's basement emergency operations center in Austin, the governor said Texas had roughly 1,000 people assigned to search-and-rescue operations across various state agencies.

Video posted to Twitter appeared to show military vehicles arriving in Port Aransas, where Harvey overturned buses, flooded streets and stripped shingles from roofs. The same day, aircrews with the U.S. Coast Guard rescued 17 people from different boats and vessels along the state's coastline, CBS News reported.

Asked Saturday afternoon about the number of deaths from the storm, Abbott said he could not confirm any fatalities and was working with local officials to gather more information.

Shelters in San Antonio and Austin were filling up with grateful Texans who had fled their homes, Abbott said, and about 1,500 evacuees were staying in state parks.

At the same time, officials in multiple cities warned of downed power lines, broken traffic lights, and streets filled with debris. Hundreds of thousands of Texans were without electricity Saturday and, in some areas, residents were asked to restrict their use of toilets and faucets because of outages at wastewater treatment plants.

The city and county of Victoria imposed a curfew on residents Saturday — lasting until 6 a.m. Sunday, and then resuming Sunday evening — to allow crews to clear hazardous debris and protect residents' safety, officials said. Elsewhere, vehicles from the Department of Transportation and other authorities were shown clearing roads and assessing damage.

Forty inches of rainfall could pour down on waterlogged areas of the state before the storm dissipates, according to the National Weather Service. Texas' primary safety concern, Abbott said Saturday, was the prospect of serious flooding.

On social media, Texans shared images of brackish waterways swollen or overflowing from the storm.

Harvey, the most powerful storm to strike Texas since 1961, first reached the Texas coastline late Friday.

The scene in Rockport, which bore much of the brunt of the storm's initial 130-mile-per-hour winds, was one of "widespread devastation," Mayor Charles Wax told CNN Saturday morning. Property damage was rampant, he said, and the loss of cellphone service and other means of communication had hampered emergency response efforts.

Local news reports from Rockport indicated many buildings were damaged overnight. After a roof collapsed at a senior housing complex, at least 10 people there were taken to a nearby jail for treatment. A portion of Rockport High School caved in.

In Fort Bend County, near Houston, county officials said a possible tornado damaged homes and downed trees, the Houston Chronicle reported. Tornadoes were also reported in Galveston and northwest Harris County. The National Weather Service issued a tornado watch for a swath of the state's coast Saturday.

Three state prisons south of Houston started to evacuate Saturday morning as Hurricane Harvey caused water levels to rise on the Brazos River, according to the Texas Department of Criminal Justice. The Ramsey, Terrell and Stringfellow prisons in Rosharon hold about 4,500 inmates total. Inmates will be moved by bus to other prison facilities in East Texas.

The state also evacuated the three prisons last May, said TDCJ spokesman Jason Clark, when flooding brought the river to record levels.

There has been minimal damage to other prison facilities in areas affected by the storm and many are running on generator power, Clark said.

Abbott announced Friday night that President Donald Trump and the Federal Emergency Management Agency, or FEMA, had approved the state's request for a disaster declaration, which includes funding to provide "individual assistance, public assistance and hazard mitigation" in Texas.

White House Press Secretary Sarah Huckabee Sanders said Friday that Trump plans to visit the state next week. ⭐

Additional reporting by Bobby Blanchard and Jolie McCullough.

Water fills the highway intersection between Interstate 59 and Highway 288 near downtown Houston on Sunday, Aug. 22, 2017. Photo by Michael Stravato

HOUSTON'S "WORST FLOOD" IS ONLY GOING TO GET WORSE

As swamped officials struggled to respond to a deadly crisis Sunday, southeast Texans were bracing for their troubles to multiply over the coming week. Harvey is on track to produce even more devastating floods.

By Kiah Collier, Neena Satija, Edgar Walters and Shannon Najmabadi | August 27, 2017

HOUSTON — As the sun set Sunday on a flood-ravaged Houston, a nagging uncertainty surrounding Tropical Storm Harvey's next move persisted.

Even 24 hours earlier, no one knew exactly how much rain the storm would bring to the sprawling metropolitan area. But meteorologists' worst case scenario ended up coming true: Harvey strengthened and dumped as much as 22 inches of rain in certain areas throughout the night and into Sunday evening, flooding countless homes, stranding families on rooftops and killing at least five people.

Scientists say the storm is likely to be the most devastating flood the Houston region has ever seen — even more so than Tropical Storm Allison in 2001, which was the worst rainstorm

The Theater District in downtown Houston on Sunday, Aug. 22, 2017. Photo by Michael Stravato

to ever befall an American city in modern history.

"The economic impact should be greater than any other flood event we've ever experienced," said Sam Brody, a scientist at a Texas A&M University at Galveston who specializes in natural hazards mitigation. "And it's going to take years for these residential communities to recover."

Late Sunday, the rainfall had let up in some areas, allowing floodwaters to drain. But it persisted in already waterlogged parts of northwest Houston and was expected to continue — if less doggedly — throughout the night and into Monday.

"It's a massive flood, and we're not out of the woods yet. This thing is going to sit here and potentially drop 10 to 15 more inches of rain," said Phil Bedient, a Rice University scientist who studies hydrology and flood prediction systems. "It is a very, very depressing situation that we find ourselves in."

A chaotic weekend

Some parts of Texas could receive up to 50 inches of rain in the coming days, an amount that would exceed state records. Two federally owned reservoirs west of Houston meant to protect the city from catastrophic flooding were already reaching historic levels as of Sunday evening. The situation will require the U.S. Army Corps of Engineers to release water down an already swollen Buffalo Bayou to protect the homes and businesses that surround the reservoirs that will certainly flood.

But just the flooding as of Sunday made for a chaotic weekend. As images posted to social media showed roads inundated with water — submerging cars and covering street signs — officials in Houston and Galveston asked

Police rescue other police and rescue workers after their city truck got stranded in high waters in downtown Houston on Sunday Aug. 27, 2017. Photo by Michael Stravato

In Houston, the 911 line received 56,000 calls between 10 p.m. Saturday and 1 p.m. Sunday, local authorities said, seven times the usual volume.

residents with high-water vehicles or boats to assist in rescue efforts.

Galveston County Judge Mark Henry said in a press conference Sunday afternoon that 25 to 35 private boat owners had responded to the call and were helping transport people to safety.

In Houston, the 911 line received 56,000 calls between 10 p.m. Saturday and 1 p.m. Sunday, local authorities said, seven times the usual volume. Earlier Sunday, Houston Mayor Sylvester Turner tweeted that Houston 911 was being overwhelmed with calls but was still functional. "There are a number of stranded people on our streets calling 911 exhausting needed resources," he wrote. "You can help by staying off the streets."

Harris County Judge Ed Emmett told the Chronicle 1,500 to 2,000 high-water rescues had been made by the county since Saturday night. And other county officials said 18 helicopters were rescuing those stranded on rooftops, after residents in flooding areas were urged to seek refuge there.

"Reports of people getting into attic to escape floodwater – do not do so unless you have an ax or means to break through onto your roof," Houston Police Chief Art Acevedo wrote on Twitter.

With emergency resources strapped, social media became a channel where pleas for rescue were issued for those trapped by flood waters that are expected to keep rising. The posts gave glimpses of the unfolding crisis and included exact addresses, names and pictures of southeast Texas' stranded residents.

One woman asked for help for a 70-year-old man trapped in a one-story house without an attic on S. Braeswood Boulevard in Houston. Another asked for help for a couple and their two cats in Dickinson, Texas.

"Please help if you can or get this information to authorities," claimed a post from twitter user Alicia Stepp. "The entire street of Colony Creek Drive needs rescue."

Yet another asked for help for 10 people, 3 dogs and two cats stuck on a roof in Dickinson. One post about a Houston family, which included a sick child, came with a picture of the people standing on their rain-soaked roof.

Henry, the Galveston County judge, said in his press conference that Dickinson was the hardest-hit part of the county, and estimated 800 to 1,200 people in the area had been rescued so far. More than a dozen nursing home residents were rescued after a viral picture showed a group of elderly people in a Dickinson facility sitting in waist-high water, according to the Chronicle.

FEMA and Trump

Outside the flood zone, state and federal officials were monitoring the situation closely.

Gov. Greg Abbott said 500 officers from the Texas Department of Public Safety had been assigned to the Houston area, and another 3,000 state and national guard members were assisting with search-and-rescue missions in various areas affected by the storm.

In Washington, D.C., at the FEMA command room near Capitol Hill, nearly 200 federal government workers and military members gathered to strategize the delivery of supplies to the hurricane-wracked region.

Televisions stations in the center were mostly tuned to the Weather Channel, but there were several big-screen feeds of local Houston affiliate stations' coverage of the damage and flooding.

Officials there emphasized that FEMA is running back-end support and following the state government's lead, and that this likely will be a years-long federal effort.

City employees pump water from city streets into Clear Lake in Nassau Bay on Saturday, Aug. 26, 2017. Photo by Michael Stravato

"The response is ongoing," said William Booher, the director of FEMA public affairs. "This is a dynamic situation ... we are coordinating very closely with our state and local partners."

A White House spokeswoman told reporters on Sunday that President Donald Trump would travel to Texas on Tuesday.

"I will be going to Texas as soon as that trip can be made without causing disruption. The focus must be life and safety," Trump tweeted Sunday morning.

"You shouldn't flood an entire city like this"

Amid days of uncertainty, many residents evacuated pre-emptively before floodwaters breached their homes. By late Sunday, about 1,000 evacuees had congregated at the George R. Brown Convention Center. City dump trucks unloaded rain-soaked evacuees in front of the center

Many were large families, carrying backpacks and rolling suitcases. Several were barefoot. Local officials expected the number of people staying there to grow to 5,000.

Christella Gomez said she packed up and left her downtown area home with her two children at the insistence of a neighbor; floodwaters from nearby Buffalo Bayou had encroached on their housing complex.

Across town, Virginia Hammond left her northwest Houston home as floodwaters began to enter — it's flooded three times in the past nine years. During another historic flood in the city last year, she found herself trapped inside with her two granddaughters as her home filled with nearly 3 feet of water.

"I kinda felt like it was gonna happen, so we left," she said in an interview Sunday afternoon.

"The streets were flooding and the bayou was up to the top."

She said she's not sure when she'll be able to return — likely when the rain stops.

Houston's always had flooding problems. It's a low-lying, coastal city built partly on swampland. But scientists, other experts and federal officials say the city's explosive growth is largely to blame for how bad flooding is now.

As millions have flocked to the metropolitan area in recent decades, local officials have largely snubbed stricter building regulations, allowing developers to pave over crucial acres of prairie land that once absorbed huge amounts of rainwater. That has led to an excess of floodwater during storms that chokes the city's vast bayou network, drainage systems and two huge federally owned reservoirs, endangering many nearby homes — including Virginia Hammond's.

"They'll always have the excuse 'Well, oh, this was the really big one,' but you shouldn't flood an entire city like this, you shouldn't have water out of banks in every single bayou like this," Bedient said. "Something is amiss and they need to rethink the whole deal, and it's not going to be cheap." ⭐

Neena Satija reports for both The Texas Tribune and Reveal.

Additional reporting by Abby Livingston and Brandon Formby.

Disclosure: Rice University has been a financial supporter of The Texas Tribune.

Elizabeth Legg hands her one-year-old daughter Reed to her husband Brian after arriving at the George R. Brown Convention Center in downtown Houston on Sunday, Aug. 27, 2017. The Leggs and other evacuees were delivered in the back of a city dump truck from Meyerland, a neighborhood hit hard by Harvey. Photo by Michael Stravato

BY ANY MEANS
NECESSARY

After Hurricane Harvey hit, Texans from near and far heeded calls from law enforcement to rescue trapped neighbors, rallying kayaks, canoes and fishing boats. In Houston, Chris Ginter took it to a whole new level – with a monster truck.

By Kiah Collier | August 30, 2017

HOUSTON — Chris Ginter propelled the monster truck cautiously but purposefully through feet-high green-brown floodwaters, past submerged mansions.

Families were surely still inside, huddled on the second story prepared to wait it out until the water receded. But as the water continued to rise and word of a mandatory evacuation began to spread, many had decided it was time to leave.

And when they did, they turned not to law enforcement or government emergency response teams but to neighbors and citizen volunteers, people who had rallied kayaks, canoes and fishing boats and formed informal bureaucracies to organize rescue missions.

Ginter's monster truck — his brother's, actually — was perhaps the most glorious rescue vessel of all, rivaled only by an imposing air boat that sent up an impressive spray from its fan as it accelerated back into the neighborhood to pick up more people. Other rescuers — mostly male — wolf-whistled at Ginter's truck

A volunteer rescues a family from their flooded house in Beaumont, Texas after Tropical Storm Harvey on Wednesday Aug. 30, 2017. (Jay Janner/Austin American-Statesman via AP)

as it glided through the water, its 55-inch tires creating a wake that angered other rescuers in smaller watercraft. "You're making me look bad, man!" enthused another rescuer with a slightly smaller truck.

After days of punishing rain from Tropical Storm Harvey, the sprawling metropolis was so waterlogged — it's being called the worst flood in U.S. history — that stretched-thin law enforcement had urged residents to use whatever means they had to rescue their neighbors. (A Harris County Flood Control District official said that as much as 30 percent of the county, home to the 600-square-mile city, was flooded by Tuesday afternoon.)

Good samaritans like Ginter, a 34-year-old commercial real estate developer and Houston native, gladly heeded the call, and by Tuesday — his third day on the job — he was clearly high on the good karma that come with repeatedly rescuing people. Strangers had gotten his cellphone number through word of mouth and called him seeking help. One caller was familiar.

"Hey, mom," said Ginter, covered in a subtle sheen of sweat, quickly informing her he had a news reporter in his truck.

"I have to make mom proud," he said, only half joking, after hanging up.

There weren't that many people left in the neighborhood who wanted to leave, Ginter said. A man standing with his family on a narrow strip of dry land between the flooded street and his garage door turned away Ginter's help, saying he was waiting for his father.

Ginter had two front seat companions — his childhood friend Robert Maguire, 34, a bar manager, and his girlfriend Gina Dyrda, 28, a bartender at a steakhouse, who Maguire had brought home from Chicago three months ago.

Ginter had borrowed his brother's truck over the weekend to rescue the couple from their swamped bayou-side townhome and they had collectively decided to keep picking people up.

As of Tuesday evening, they had rescued at least 50 people, said Dyrda, a petite and enthusiastic brunette with a cupcake tattoo behind her right ear. There were lots of dogs and babies, including twin girls screaming their heads off, she said. The crew had been out until 10 p.m. the night before.

"Last night was sad — very sad — because we couldn't fit everyone," Maguire said. They had been worried about getting stuck in one of the prolific manholes whose covers had floated away, but didn't think they had encountered one yet. They weren't sure if even the monster tires could traverse them.

They dropped their evacuees on the dry end of a boulevard abutting the neighborhood, wedged between a strip mall with a dentist's office and a Sylvia's Enchilada Kitchen, where citizen volunteers helped evacuees down from the truck with a step ladder. Others waded out into knee-deep water to pull in smaller boats.

Dozens of onlookers had gathered there by Tuesday evening, a crowd representative of the most racially and ethnically diverse major city in the U.S. — black, white, Latino, east and southeast Asian. A young South American couple casually sipped yerba mate from a stainless steel straw and mug.

Many of them lived nearby and were wondering if the rising waters would eventually reach their own homes. Even though the rain had let up and nagging gray clouds had moved aside, revealing bright blue skies, water levels were continuing to rise with the U.S. Army Corps of Engineers releasing water from upstream reservoirs to help minimize flooding of homes around the detention ponds. They had upped the release rate, and were considering releasing even more into an already swollen Buffalo Bayou, which many of the homes in the neighborhood backed up to.

The onlookers gawked somberly as boats arrived filled with blank-faced senior citizens —

Residents near Buffalo Bayou in western Houston are evacuated by boat on Tuesday, August 29, 2017. Photo by Pu Ying Huang

hovered over by worried adult children — and families with teary-eyed mothers. They carried rolling suitcases, trash bags stuffed with clothes and pet carriers with anxious dogs and cats.

Some were calm, or maybe just in shock. Others even looked annoyed. Many had never flooded before.

And many hadn't wanted to leave — even a woman caring for her father who needed dialysis the next day.

Emily, who teaches math at a private Christian school and refused to give her last name, said she had been "prepared to live on beans, indefinitely," even as water steadily flowed into her garage. The power had been out and she was all alone — her husband was on a business trip and her two kids were away at college. Then a neighbor arrived and told her there was a mandatory evacuation for the area and citizen rescuers were starting to leave the neighborhood, having scooped up almost everyone who wanted to leave.

"Every house was like its own island," Emily said.

While poorer areas were surely harder hit, the scene that played out near the posh neighborhood was evidence that Harvey did not discriminate. Still, Dyrdra said many evacuees told her they had no place to go. Surely some would hitch a ride to a hotel. Others with fewer means would head to one of several shelters that had popped up around the city. They had at least made it this far.

In retrospect, it would be a good thing. By the next day, floodwaters had risen in the neighborhood by several more feet. ⭐

Neena Satija contributed to this report.

A volunteer rescues a family from their flooded house in Beaumont, Texas after Tropical Storm Harvey on Wednesday Aug. 30, 2017. A weaker Harvey replicated its devastating roll Wednesday, returning to shore with a deluge of rain that inundated homes and highways and left police and government officials struggling to pluck people from the water.(Jay Janner/Austin American-Statesman via AP

Residents evacuate their homes near the Addicks Reservoir as floodwaters from Tropical Storm Harvey rise Tuesday, Aug. 29, 2017, in Houston. (AP Photo/ David J. Phillip)

COASTAL TEXAS COUNTY'S LONG RECOVERY BEGINS

Nowhere was Hurricane Harvey's devastation felt more than Aransas County, which has had one storm-related death and has had many buildings severely damaged.

By Brandon Formby | August 26, 2017

ROCKPORT — As Ruben Sazon waited out Hurricane Harvey in his apartment Friday, he was certain that his roof was going to be ripped off.

"The howl of the wind was amazing," he said, adding that "it came in with a roar."

The roof stayed in place. But the Category 4 hurricane did enough structural damage to make his home uninhabitable, leaving Sazon with no place of his own and uncertainty about what he'll do next.

"This is the history-making hurricane," Sazon said Saturday of the storm that pummeled the area he has called home for more than two decades. "This is the one people will always be talking about."

Across this battered nook of the Texas coastline, Aransas County and its residents are beginning the difficult work of installing order and a sense of normalcy after Hurricane Harvey's brutal arrival the night before. But unrelenting rain and wind from the massive storm are muddling those initial efforts.

Emergency personnel poured into Aransas County on Saturday and began assessing this normally laid-back coastal community's damage, which included complete loss of power, hundreds of millions of dollars in property damage and an untold number of impassable roads.

The seemingly random scattershot of destruction — decimated buildings, snapped

A Texas flag flies above wreckage in Port Aransas from Hurricane Harvey on Wednesday, Aug. 30, 2017. Photo by Bob Daemmrich

51

"This is the history-making hurricane. This the one people will always be talking about."

power poles, downed trees — alongside completely intact structures leads officials to believe that tornadoes came with the storm.

"It's evident the way the damage is," Aransas County Judge C.H. "Burt" Mills Jr. said Saturday.

At least one person died in a house fire that officials didn't discover until after Harvey moved through. Emergency calls couldn't be made or answered during the brunt of the storm's impact. About 40 percent of the 24,500 people who call Aransas County home defied a mandatory evacuation order and stayed behind. So far, only 12 to 14 people with non-life-threatening injuries required medical attention. But local, state and federal officials on Saturday had just started arduous search-and-rescue efforts to aid anyone trapped.

They plan to evacuate those in damaged homes who can't leave on their own.

"We don't have a place to put them," Mills said. "We can't take care of them."

Despite a cavalry of regional, state and federal responders, the county's inundated infrastructure and lack of power left local leaders unable to estimate when the tens of thousands who fled in a highway-clogging

Donations are sorted and distributed as cleanup begins in Port Aransas, Texas on Wednesday, Aug. 30, 2017. Photo by Bob Daemmrich exodus ahead of the storm will be able to return home.

For now, officials want them to stay out. Expectations that the rain will last days forebode worsening conditions. And as the county's tiny beach towns begin the early stages of recovery, Harvey's large size and slow movement will continue to threaten other parts of the state with flood damage likely to require great demand for response resources.

Still, county leaders remained optimistic that the area will be restored and rebuilt. Fulton Mayor Jimmy Kendrick said residents love their community. As he surveyed damage early in the day, he stumbled across parishioners of a damaged church already cleaning up.

"We are one," he said.

"Devastating"

Ahead of the storm, Sazon, an artist and jeweler, placed his sofa upright to block the doorway to his living room, where mattress box springs blocked a sliding glass door to his second-floor apartment's balcony.

Harvey's merciless winds broke every window in his apartment.

"All you could hear was things hitting, glass breaking," Toni Castillo, Sazon's girlfriend, said of the storm.

On Saturday morning, Sazon headed to downtown Rockport to check on the studio where he paints, makes jewelry and sells his work. What had been a small, waterfront building with a turquoise awning facing the town's shop-lined Austin Street was essentially nothing more than an intact roof sitting atop a pile of collapsed rubble.

Sazon, who rented his apartment and the building where he ran Sazon Studio and Gallery, didn't have insurance for either. With no cellphone service, Sazon and his girlfriend didn't have a way to call relatives or friends.

They planned to drive about 30 miles west to Corpus Christi and stay with his daughter. From there, they hoped to figure out what to do next.

"It's devastating to me," he said from his car in front of what had been the studio.

Hope amid concern

Troy and Laurie Rodgers had retired to a condo on Aransas Bay after spending decades vacationing in the small town. As Harvey approached, they decided to leave. Troy Rodgers left Friday, hours before Harvey made landfall. But Laurie Rodgers headed out the night before. The drive to Austin, where her sister lives, took eight hours, more than double the time it usually does. Cars were bumper to bumper for the first hour out of town.

"Every gas station was packed," she said. "The traffic was terrible."

Their condo is a block from downtown, where a spattering of satellite trucks was parked Saturday so television reporters could do national broadcasts. The couple, like others who fled ahead of the storm, spent Saturday watching the coverage in shock over the damage reports.

"We kind of joke around and then all of a sudden something will hit and I'm just trying not to cry," Laurie Rodgers said. "The reality of it is kind of overwhelming."

Like local leaders, Laurie Rodgers is hopeful despite the continuing waves of concern.

"I think it will be fine," she said. "I think people will ... choose to stay and rebuild." ★

Shannon Najmabadi contributed to this report.

Extensive damage from Hurricane Harvey litters Port Aransas on Wednesday, Aug. 30, 2017. Photo by Bob Daemmrich

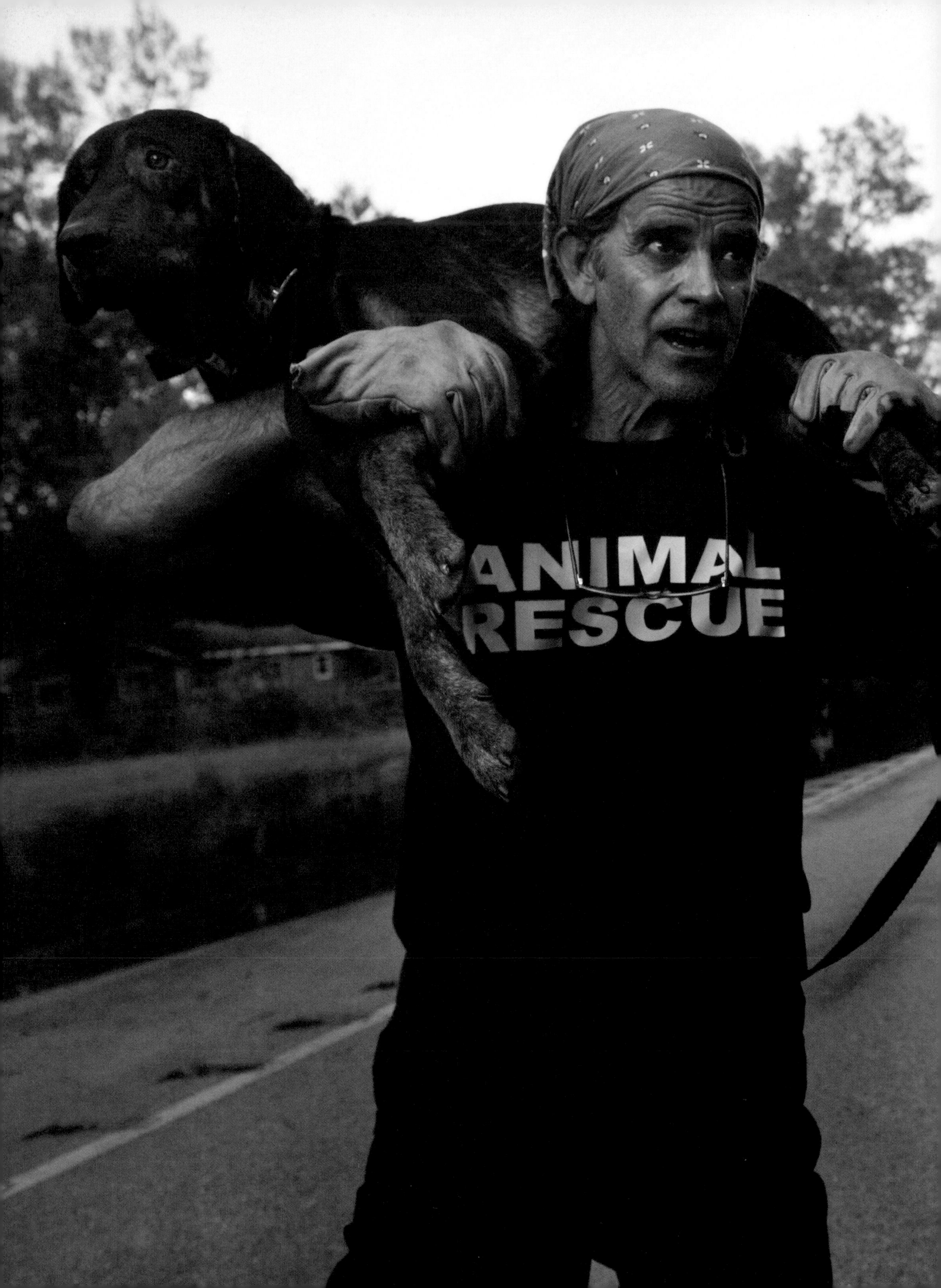
ANIMAL
RESCUE

Animal rescuer Peter Crowe from Virginia, who also volunteered during Hurricane Katrina, carries a stranded dog to safety on Sept. 3, 2017, in Vidor, Texas. (Newcom)

HARVEY'S WINDS AND RAIN
DISRUPT TEXAS AGRICULTURE

Hurricane Harvey did more than transform cityscape by turning highways into rivers; it also upended life for farmers and ranchers across dozens of counties that Gov. Greg Abbott declared disaster zones.

By Jim Malewitz | August 30, 2017

Like many of his neighbors, Robby Reed had high hopes for his cotton fields in 2017.

"It was going to be my best cotton crop year ever," said Reed, who raises a variety of crops on some 2,500 acres outside of Bay City, about 80 miles southwest of Houston. "Everybody was making big cotton crops."

Then along came Harvey.

Cotton crop ruined by Harvey in Refugio County, about 6 miles south of Refugio on US 77, on Wednesday, Aug. 30, 2017. Photo by Bob Daemmrich

High-speed winds ripped apart cotton modules – large blocks of unprocessed cotton – leaving them strewn about fields and gin yards.

The hurricane-turned-tropical storm devastated a wide swath along Texas' Coastal Bend. Flooding from the relentless rains sent five feet of water into Reed's two-story house and swamped his only partially harvested cotton fields.

"Everything else is just, you know, kind of wasted," the 39-year-old said this week.

Harvey did more than transform cityscape by turning highways into rivers; it also upended life for farmers and ranchers across dozens of counties that Gov. Greg Abbott declared disaster zones. The powerful winds and rains destroyed crops, displaced livestock and disrupted trade.

Texas typically exports nearly one-fourth of the country's wheat and a major portion of its corn and soybeans, according to the state Department of Agriculture, but a shutdown of ports ahead of Harvey halted export.

At least 1.2 million beef cows graze in 54 counties Abbott had added to his disaster list as of Tuesday, according to Texas A&M AgriLife Extension Service. State and industry officials did not immediately have data on how many were lost, but news reports and social media have circulated images of wandering cattle and dramatic rescues of the animals from floodwaters.

"There have been a lot of wonderful stories going around on social media of people banding together to help save one another's livestock," Agriculture Commissioner Sid Miller said in statement. "I want to send a great big thank you to these folks for doing things the Texas way, which is to be a great neighbor and help those in need."

Harvey also affected cropland. Texas rice producers had already harvested about 75 percent of the year's rice crop, according to the Agriculture Department, but wind and water likely damaged storage bins, leading to more crop losses.

Harvey hit cotton farmers like Reed particularly hard, destroying their prospects of a banner year. While the region's crops — corn, for instance, were out of the ground before the storm hit, cotton was another story.

"A lot of cotton didn't get harvested," said Gene Hall, a spokesman for the Texas Farm Bureau. "We know that they were racing the clock trying to beat landfall ... I think anything left on the stalk, you got to consider that a total loss."

In Matagorda County, for instance, just 70 percent of cotton had been harvested, while only 35 percent was out of the ground in Wharton County, Hall said.

What's more, high-speed winds ripped apart cotton modules — large blocks of unprocessed cotton — leaving them strewn about fields and gin yards.

Reed said the floodwaters had kept him from even being able to survey the damage to some of his land near Matagorda Bay, and that he planned to soon take a ride in his buddy's helicopter to take a look.

Though Reed said his family would ultimately "be alright" after rebuilding and replanting, they wouldn't forget this setback. ★

Disclosure: The Texas Farm Bureau and Texas A&M AgriLife Extension Service have been financial supporters of The Texas Tribune.

Cattle are stranded in a flooded pasture on Highway 71 in La Grange, Texas, after Hurricane Harvey on Monday, Aug. 28, 2017. (Jay Janner/Austin American-Statesman via AP)

Volunteers from Texas A&M help rescue horses along the south Sam Houston Tollway, Tuesday, Aug. 29, 2017, in Houston, following Tropical Storm Harvey. (Mark Mulligan/Houston Chronicle via AP)

TRUMP VISITS
CORPUS CHRISTI, AUSTIN TO SEE HARVEY RECOVERY

President Donald Trump was in Texas Tuesday to see the recovery efforts underway in the aftermath of Hurricane Harvey.

By Patrick Svitek | August 29, 2017

President Donald Trump visited Texas on Tuesday to see the recovery efforts underway in the aftermath of Hurricane Harvey, the first major natural disaster to strike the United States under his leadership.

In visits to Corpus Christi and Austin, Trump marveled at the massive impact of the storm, describing it as "epic" and "historic" in briefings with state officials. He set the bar high for his administration's response to Harvey, saying he wants it to be used as a model for the country long after Texas' recovery.

"We want to do it better than ever before," Trump said in Corpus Christi. "We want to be looked at in five years, in 10 years from now as, this is the way to do it."

Trump's day in Texas began Tuesday morning in Corpus Christi, the city along the Gulf Coast near where Harvey made landfall Friday as a Category 4 storm. Trump made a stop at a local firehouse for a roundtable with local and state officials, and when it was over, he emerged to a crowd of hundreds of people outside.

"What a crowd, what a turnout," he said, taking in the scene as he stood between two

President Donald Trump and first lady Melania Trump walk from Marine One to board Air Force One at Andrews Air Force Base, Maryland, Tuesday, Aug. 29, 2017, for a trip to Texas to get an update on Hurricane Harvey relief efforts. (AP Photo/Evan Vucci)

65

fire trucks. "I will tell you, this is historic, it's epic, what happened. But you know what, it happened in Texas, and Texas can handle anything."

Trump then pulled out a Texas flag, getting loud cheers from the crowd.

Hours later in Austin, Trump continued to express awe at Harvey's wrath as he paid a visit to the state's Emergency Operations Center. After praising workers at the center for staying on top of the storm and its aftermath, Trump attended a briefing with state officials where he mused about how unassuming the storm seemed.

"It sounds like such an innocent name," Trump said of Harvey. "But it's not. It's not innocent."

At the briefing, Trump also braced members of Congress for a "costly proposition" in coming up with an aid package for the storm. Afterward, U.S. Sen. John Cornyn, R-Texas, told reporters he's suggested a "down payment" on Harvey aid to White House officials and they have been "sympathetic" to such a plan.

Trump did not see much wreckage during the trip, with the firehouse being his only stop in Corpus Christi and the Emergency Operations his only stop in Austin. As Trump headed to Texas on Tuesday morning, Sarah Huckabee Sanders, the White House press secretary, told reporters that Trump wanted to be "very cautious about making sure that any activity doesn't disrupt any of the recovery efforts that are still ongoing."

Trump was joined throughout Tuesday by Gov. Greg Abbott and First Lady Melania Trump. The first lady did not deliver remarks in Corpus Christi or Austin but issued a statement afterward saying, "What I found most profound during the visit was not only the strength and resilience of the people of Texas, but the compassion and sense of community that has taken over the State."

Abbott, for his part, heaped praise on Trump and his administration for taking the storm seriously early on and moving quickly to respond once it hit Texas. Abbott also sought to portray Trump as a compassionate leader behind the scenes, recalling in Austin how the two had watched images of drenched Houston on their flight from Corpus Christi. "The president was heartbroken about what he saw," Abbott said.

Abbott was not the only Texas elected official who turned out for Trump's trip. He was joined at points throughout the day by Lt. Gov. Dan Patrick, Cornyn, U.S. Sen. Ted Cruz and several other members of Congress.

Trump brought with him a number of Cabinet officials whose departments are involved in the recovery effort. They included Elaine Duke, acting secretary of the Department of Homeland Security; Ben Carson, secretary of the Department of Housing and Urban Development; and Tom Price, secretary of the Department of Health and Human Services.

Trump's trip Tuesday likely will not be the only time he visits Texas this week. Huckabee Sanders told reporters he intends to return Saturday to see a "different part of the state."

Vice President Mike Pence, in a radio interview Tuesday morning, said he and his wife will visit southeast Texas later this week. ☆

A Trump supporter chops firewood as he prepares for a possible visit by U.S. President Donald Trump as storm damage hampers relief efforts in Rockport about 30 miles north of Corpus Christi, three days after the historic Category 4 storm made landfall along the Texas Coast. Photo by Bob Daemmrich

A MAGNET FOR GROWTH...AND FLOODING

Northwest Houston suburbs like Cypress have exploded in population in recent years. Scientists say that's a big reason some neighborhoods here saw devastating floods last year and now from Hurricane Harvey.

By Neena Satija | August 31, 2017

CYPRESS — Now that the waters have receded, the peaceful scene at the Stable Gate Subdivision is a deceiving one. Upon driving in after days of rain from Hurricane Harvey, the mostly brick single-family houses seem intact, the streets appear free of water, and cars roam freely.

But look a little closer, and signs of the devastation come into focus. Wet carpet is strewn out onto nearly every front yard. Some yards are piled with plastic bags, drywall, and even doors. And just a short drive away, the streets suddenly turn into rivers.

"I don't have time to talk," said Stacey Summers, a Stable Gate resident the Texas Tribune and ProPublica first spoke to last year — after her home had taken in more than a foot of water in the devastating "Tax Day" floods of April 2016.

During those floods, Summers and almost everyone in her neighborhood saw their homes take in water, and many had to evacuate by boat. Most had never seen their homes flood in the area's 15-year history, prompting local media to proclaim, "Subdivision never flooded, until it did, and residents want answers."

A Harris County Sheriff's deputy rescues two children from high floodwaters brought on by Hurricane Harvey in the Blackhorse subdivision in Cypress, Texas, on August 27, 2017. (Newscom)

But scientists say residents of Stable Gate, and those neighborhoods surrounding them, have long been sitting ducks for this type of event. And just a year and a half after the Tax Day floods ripped through these communities, Hurricane Harvey has dumped even more rain on the area. Summers' home once again flooded; piles of drywall, a Shop-Vac and what appeared to be brand new doors removed from their hinges sat in her front yard.

The Texas Tribune and ProPublica profiled this northwest Houston suburb of Cypress last year to highlight how development in the region is contributing to more severe flooding.

Danny Gabriel, who also owns a home in Stable Gate, has seen that firsthand. He bought the house in 2003, and it's now flooded two years in a row, during Tax Day last year and then Harvey — even though it is not officially in a floodplain. (Luckily, Gabriel bought flood insurance anyway. "I'm from Louisiana, so I know about flooding," he said.)

The first time there was any kind of "water event" after he moved, Gabriel remembered, water "came up to the sidewalk. The next time, it came up to my yard. Then the next time it came up to the walkway, and then, with the Tax Day flood it came in. And it was just getting worse and worse and worse." Harvey's rain sent about 7 inches of water into his house.

Because all the water in this area drains into Cypress Creek, it's called the Cypress Creek watershed. And scientists say the increased frequency and severity of floods that residents are experiencing is in part because of explosive growth here. That growth has paved over much of the pasture and prairie land there that once absorbed floodwaters. It's also occurred in and near known floodplains — which experts say is dangerous and irresponsible.

In the 1990s, as the population started to climb, two major floods hit the area — both considered "500-year" events, which should have just a 1 in 500 chance of occurring in any given year. The Tax Day floods of April 2016 once again caused portions of the area to reach 500-year flood levels. And during Harvey, official readings showed that some parts of Cypress Creek got high enough to surpass all of those previous records.

Growth accelerated after Tropical Storm Allison in 2001, which had been the worst rainstorm to befall Houston until Harvey dethroned it. (Stable Gate, for instance, was built post-Allison.) Between 2000 and 2010, the Cypress Creek watershed's population grew by nearly 70 percent to a population of 587,142 — equivalent to that of Milwaukee. But some neighborhoods existed long before that and had also never flooded until now. They are not officially in floodplains, and so many residents didn't buy flood insurance — like Matt Turner and his wife, Laura.

When the couple bought their decades-old house in Cypress five years ago, "the house technically wasn't in the floodplain at the time," Turner explained. Then, after water came into their yard during the Tax Day flood last year, they discussed buying insurance but never got around to it. Now it's too late; 8-10 inches of water seeped into their home earlier this week and it will likely cost them tens of thousands of dollars to repair.

"As soon as we can, we're getting flood insurance," Turner said, as friends wielding hammers and other heavy-duty tools helped him and his wife tear out the entire first floor of the home. Over the past few days, Turner said he's started to learn more about a local group called the Cypress Creek Flood Control Coalition, which has advocated for smarter growth in the area since the 1990s.

"We keep on tearing up the ground and putting concrete on it," Turner said. "My fear is that six months from now, everybody kind of forgets ... politicians forget, citizens forget."

Floodwaters from Hurricane Harvey fill the streets of Bellaire in Harris County, Texas on August 27, 2017. (Newscom)

Dick Smith, the founder of the coalition, told the Texas Tribune and ProPublica last year that he couldn't even convince county officials to at least plan for the impacts of explosive growth in the region.

Smith, who also lives in Cypress, could not be reached on Wednesday. His home was under several feet of water and neighbors said they believe he evacuated.

The U.S. Army Corps of Engineers and county officials have been talking for years about managing growth in the Cypress Creek watershed. Both agencies have research to show that development there may have made flooding worse for the region. That includes research into a phenomenon that forces some excess rainfall in the area into Addicks and Barker Reservoirs — massive basins that were built in the 1940s to protect central and west Houston.

But a push for growth in northwest Harris County — which has some of the last remaining undeveloped land in the Houston region — has made serious discussions about the issue difficult. Officials would like to change development regulations there and even build another reservoir to hold excess floodwaters, but they've made little progress despite years of talks.

For now, Danny Gabriel says he thinks there have been some improvements to the Stable Gate subdivision since the Tax Day floods. He believes that small projects to improve nearby drainage are one reason his home actually took in less water in it than during the Tax Day flood — even though Harvey dumped far more rain onto his neighborhood.

Still — he's ready to get out. He's already bought a new house in a neighborhood west of Stable Gate, on ground that's 15 feet higher. "We're high and dry back there," he said, although the new home is trapped between two impassable waterways right now.

The next challenge will be selling his old house. But he's hopeful. Gabriel said he and his wife just met a real estate agent in the neighborhood who recently sold her own house after it flooded during Tax Day, and has sold 4-6 more homes in the area.

"She told us, get [our house] fixed up," Gabriel recalled. "I'll be able to sell it." ⭐

Neena Satija reports for both The Texas Tribune and Reveal.

Kiah Collier contributed reporting.

Debris is removed from a house on Stable Oak Drive following Harvey on August 30, 2017. (Newscom)

HISTORICALLY BLACK NEIGHBORHOODS DEVASTATED BY FLOODING, WITH LITTLE SAFETY NET

Houston's historically black neighborhoods were hit hard by Hurricane Harvey – and many don't have the safety net that residents in other parts of town can rely on to recover.

By Neena Satija and Kiah Collier | August 31, 2017

HOUSTON — Six-year-old Karla Rogers lingered on the sidewalk outside her apartment in the hot sun on Thursday, refusing to go any farther. Her friend had told her there were snakes inside.

Five days earlier, her father had lowered her down from a second-story window into the arms of a Houston police officer standing in chest-deep floodwater that had appeared almost overnight with the arrival of what by then had become Tropical Storm Harvey.

"She's been devastated ever since," said Eddie Rogers, who is 50. "My main concern was just getting her out."

They returned to their public housing complex Thursday afternoon to meet with a FEMA inspector who would do a walkthrough of the three-bedroom, one-bath dwelling and

Workers throw away debris and ruined possessions at a public housing project near Buffalo Bayou in Houston on Thursday, Aug. 31, 2017. Photo by Michael Stravato

75

determine if they qualified for financial assistance that would allow them to get a hotel room. When they arrived, the complex was nearly deserted — a lot of other people had gotten help, Rogers said — and the inspector was running late.

They had to walk a mile from the downtown emergency shelter where they had been staying for nearly a week because their Ford Explorer had been flooded out, Rogers said.

"So we can't get in our car no more?" a wide-eyed Karla asked, her cheeks gleaming with tears.

"No, baby," he said.

When he picked her up to carry her toward the apartment, she burst into tears and began to shriek: "I'm scared; I don't want to go!" The inspector had just called and would arrive in 15 minutes.

The scene at Rogers' apartment complex was playing out all over Houston's Fifth Ward, which has long been a predominantly black neighborhood. First settled by freed slaves in the mid-1800s, the Fifth Ward and nearby neighborhoods were once thriving communities of railroad and industrial workers in the mid-20th century. But the decline of industry in the neighborhood and a lack of government investment helped contribute to rapid deterioration later on.

Not all of the area is known to flood regularly; some newer homes and apartments escaped the waters even during Harvey. FEMA doesn't consider Rogers' complex to be in a floodplain even though it backs right up to Buffalo Bayou, a usually slow-moving river that runs through downtown Houston but which swelled to unprecedented levels during the storm.

"This was the big one," said Rev. James Caldwell, a community advocate who grew up in the Fifth Ward and has lived here for the past 20 years. "This is the first time that I'm aware of in years that this area actually flooded into homes. It floods — the streets turn into rivers, and all that — but the homes themselves are generally safe. This time, it hit homes."

Compared to other parts of town, the safety net for many of these residents is severely lacking. Rogers and his daughter had moved to their public housing complex just two months earlier from a homeless shelter in League City. He had lost his job and his apartment after divorcing Karla's mother, and he fought a long custody battle to keep his daughter.

All over the Fifth Ward, the watermark appeared to be waist-deep in the one-story homes. Yards were full of debris and wet carpet. Many residents who had been flooded out were walking to and from their houses each day to a downtown evacuee shelter — about 4 miles away — to get food and a dry place to sleep.

In wealthy neighborhoods, many residents had kayaks and fishing boats to help rescue their neighbors. But that wasn't the case in one apartment complex just north of the Fifth Ward.

Marilyn Wilson, 61, watches as volunteers Jamal Stenson and his son Aahmad clean her flooded apartment out in the Kashmere Gardens neighborhood of Houston on Thursday, Aug. 31, 2017. Photo by Michael Stravato

Water had gotten up to 18-year-old Kisha Adams' waist in her family's one-story apartment before she sought refuge in the upstairs unit with neighbors. But the water kept rising. Then, the breaker box across the parking lot of the rundown complex caught fire, and Adams watched the smoke and flames as she called 911.

She never got through. Helicopters flew overhead and she tried to wave huge flashlights in their direction, but they never stopped. So Adams, her parents and her 1-year-old daughter waited nervously with no power and spoiling food until the water receded. It took two and half days for them to walk safely downstairs.

"We lost everything," said Adams, a native Houstonian. "Everybody lost everything."

Just a few doors down, 61-year-old Marilyn Wilson put her head in her hands as neighbors hauled all of her ruined possessions — furniture, clothes, heirlooms, electronics — from her apartment. They wore masks over their faces to protect from a toxic smell that seemed to permeate the area.

Wilson has a number of severe health problems, including diabetes and high blood pressure, and she usually gets around in a wheelchair. After the water receded in her home, she returned to discover all her medical equipment was ruined. That includes a machine that helps her with sleep apnea and a hospital-style electric bed that keeps her elevated since she cannot lie flat. She said Medicare will replace the items for free but that she doesn't know how long that will take.

"It was hell. It was hell on earth, I'm telling you," said Wilson as she recalled the experience. "I wouldn't wish this on anybody because this is devastating." A retired cafeteria worker, Wilson takes in just $1,000 a month from a combination of social security and retirement income, more than half of which she spends on rent.

Caldwell said Wilson's story is not an unusual one for the area. Many residents here, including seniors and disabled people, were trapped during the storm and are now facing what seems like an impossible task: rebuilding mostly one-story apartments and finding somewhere else to live in the meantime. They will have to rely on FEMA for aid, and it may take months for that help to come through.

By mid-week, residents across the city were taking first steps in the rebuilding process — ripping out soggy carpet, running big fans to help dry things out — but they appeared much wearier in the Fifth Ward area than wealthier parts of town.

Hundreds of families have been displaced from city-owned public housing complexes that flooded in the wake of Harvey, said Brian Gage, a senior policy adviser for the Houston Housing Authority. Rebuilding will be a long and painful process for people with so few resources, he said while standing inside a cavernous hall at the downtown convention center where Rogers and his daughter had been staying.

About 90 of the 296 units in Rogers' 1950s-era complex had flooded, according to two maintenance men cruising around the complex in a dirt-crusted golf cart.

By Thursday evening, the FEMA inspector had looked at Rogers' home, and he'd walked with his daughter back to their evacuee shelter. They had hoped that federal aid might come through quickly, but the inspector told him it would be days before they could get back with him.

Even though the situation seemed dire, Rogers appeared calm. He was doing everything for Karla.

"I've got to keep fighting. This is my reason to," he said, gesturing toward her. ⭐

Neena Satija reports for both The Texas Tribune and Reveal.

Peter Smith, Robert Lester, Jr., Tierell Goodman, left to right, dispose of damaged drywall and insulation from a flooded home in Beaumont on Monday, Sept. 4, 2017. Wearing masks and gloves, they work to clean out damaged materials before mold settles in. Photo by Pu Ying Huang

SHELTERS REMAIN A LIFELINE FOR THOUSANDS

More than 10,000 people remain in Houston shelters, where Texans rescued from rising waters figure out their next steps and search for provisions.

By Kiah Collier, Neena Satija and Brandon Formby | August 31, 2017

HOUSTON — Anthony Moore stood amid thousands of this city's displaced residents and scores of volunteers at the George R. Brown Convention Center on Thursday and clung to a garbage bag filled with toys, shirts and diapers.

The 37-year-old spent days trapped in his flooded northeastern Houston house where he lives with his wife, two children and grandmother. But after they ran out of water, Moore decided he and his wife should leave everyone else behind and walk more than eight miles to get supplies at one of dozens of shelters for Hurricane Harvey evacuees.

"I said, 'Baby, let's try and make it,'" said Moore, who wore a black baseball cap that said "H-Town."

Between 6,500 and 8,000 people remained at the convention center Thursday, days after Harvey slammed into the coast as a catastrophic Category 4 hurricane and then dumped epic amounts of rainfall on southeast Texas after lessening into a tropical storm.

As floodwaters recede and the extent of the unprecedented damage comes into sharper focus, many will have to stay in the city's shelters for an indefinite amount of time. One woman who was among the first to arrive at the convention center has already found a job cleaning the building.

"I'm just grateful and thankful for, you know, what they've done here," said the woman,

Evacuees get snacks at the George R. Brown Convention Center in Houston on Sunday, Aug. 27, 2017. Photo by Michael Stravato

who got separated from reporters amid the building's bustle before she could give her name.

The convention center was part dorm, part animal shelter, part counseling center. Volunteers checked people in. Stacks of donated food, clothes and diapers peppered the large exhibit spaces. County housing authority employees scoured the building and other shelters Thursday in the hopes of finding public housing tenants, who are among the city's most vulnerable residents and who scattered during the storm's early chaos.

Many of the people who fled to the shelters amid the merciless rain have begun to return home, head to other cities or find friends and family with dry rooms to spare. Others, like Moore, are still showing up in search of food, water and clothing.

"The volunteers have been real nice," Moore said.

At the height of the state's still-unfolding crisis, more than 10,000 people flocked to this building in downtown Houston. It's one of seven shelters that the city, Harris County and Red Cross are jointly operating. Nonprofits and churches have opened dozens more, but county officials are transferring people from smaller buildings to NRG Stadium southwest of downtown.

That facility had 2,300 people Thursday, but can hold 10,000.

"It's just a lot more comfortable and effective than putting up cots in a school gymnasium," said Joe Stinebaker, communications director for Harris County Judge Ed Emmett.

And with Hurricane Irma gathering strength in the Atlantic Ocean and another storm brewing in the Gulf of Mexico, officials say the larger shelters are likely to become mainstays for the foreseeable future.

"We're certainly not going to take any chances, shut it down, then have another storm and have to gear it all up again," Stinebaker said.

Evacuees and volunteers line up at the George R. Brown Convention Center in downtown Houston on Thursday, Aug. 31, 2017. Photo by Michael Stravato

Cities throughout the state have also turned convention centers and other large facilities into makeshift homes for those who fled the storm and its subsequent floods.

Haley Gray and her family arrived at the Houston convention center early this week after their Channelview home flooded.

"It was almost like a river," she said.

She and her sister's seven children were rescued by a helicopter and have been at the shelter for four days. On Thursday, they were relocating to a hotel. From there, they'll begin to figure out what to do next. Gray is on disability and helps take care of her sister's kids, ages 1 to 11. The family's car was likely totaled in the flood. Most of their belongings were ruined. Like many, they must now chart a new life with few resources and a cloud of uncertainty hanging over their heads.

"I don't think we're going to be able to go back because it's pretty bad," she said as her nieces and nephews crowded around her.

Moore and his wife, meanwhile, planned to spend the rest of the day figuring out how to get back home with the donations they collected. Moore tried calling 911 when the water rose, but was told he'd be put on a waiting list for rescue. Help never came.

As they collected supplies, their two kids and Moore's grandmother waited in a waterlogged house. Moore, who is a carpenter, hopes a friend will pump most of the water out. He'll sweep out the rest, then get to work making the house habitable again.

"So I'm just going to try and do everything over," he said. ✪

Neena Satija reports for both The Texas Tribune and Reveal.

Giulia Afiune contributed to this report.

Ayub Karovalla, Snisha Bhandari and Almas Maredian (left to right) sort donated goods in the Houston Food Bank carousel room on Wednesday, Aug. 30, 2017. Photo by Pu Ying Huang

Anna Ucheomumu, left, high fives Houston Texans defensive end J.J. Watt after loading a car with relief supplies to people impacted by Hurricane Harvey on Sunday, Sept. 3, 2017, in Houston. Watt's Hurricane Harvey Relief Fund has raised millions of dollars to help those affected by the storm. (Brett Coomer/Houston Chronicle via AP, Pool)

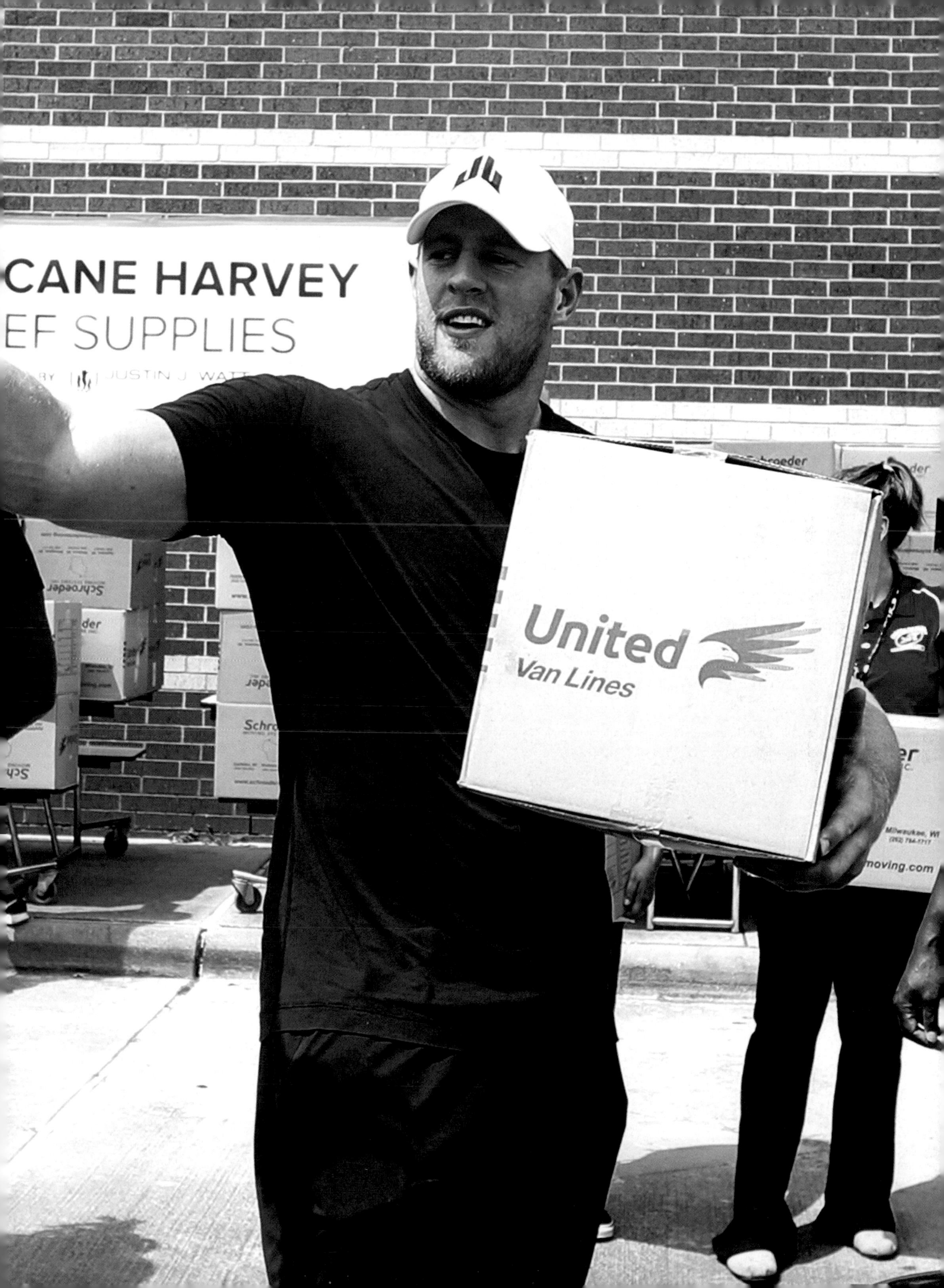
CANE HARVEY
EF SUPPLIES
United
Van Lines

Bob Daemmrich

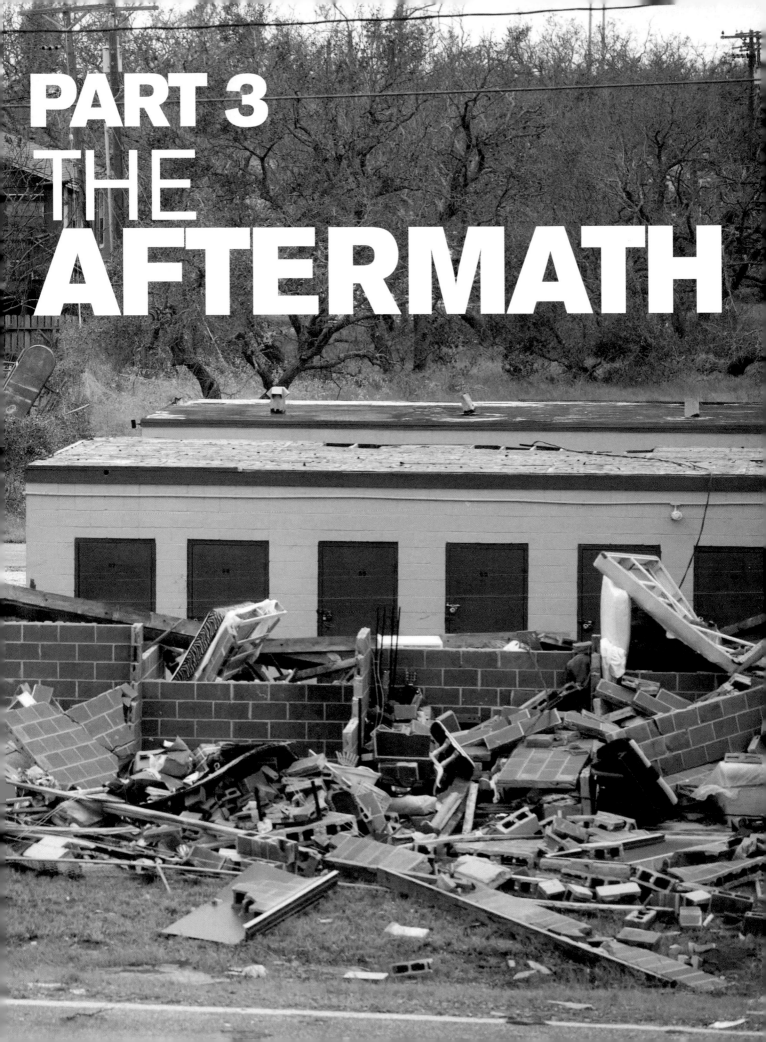

PART 3
THE
AFTERMATH

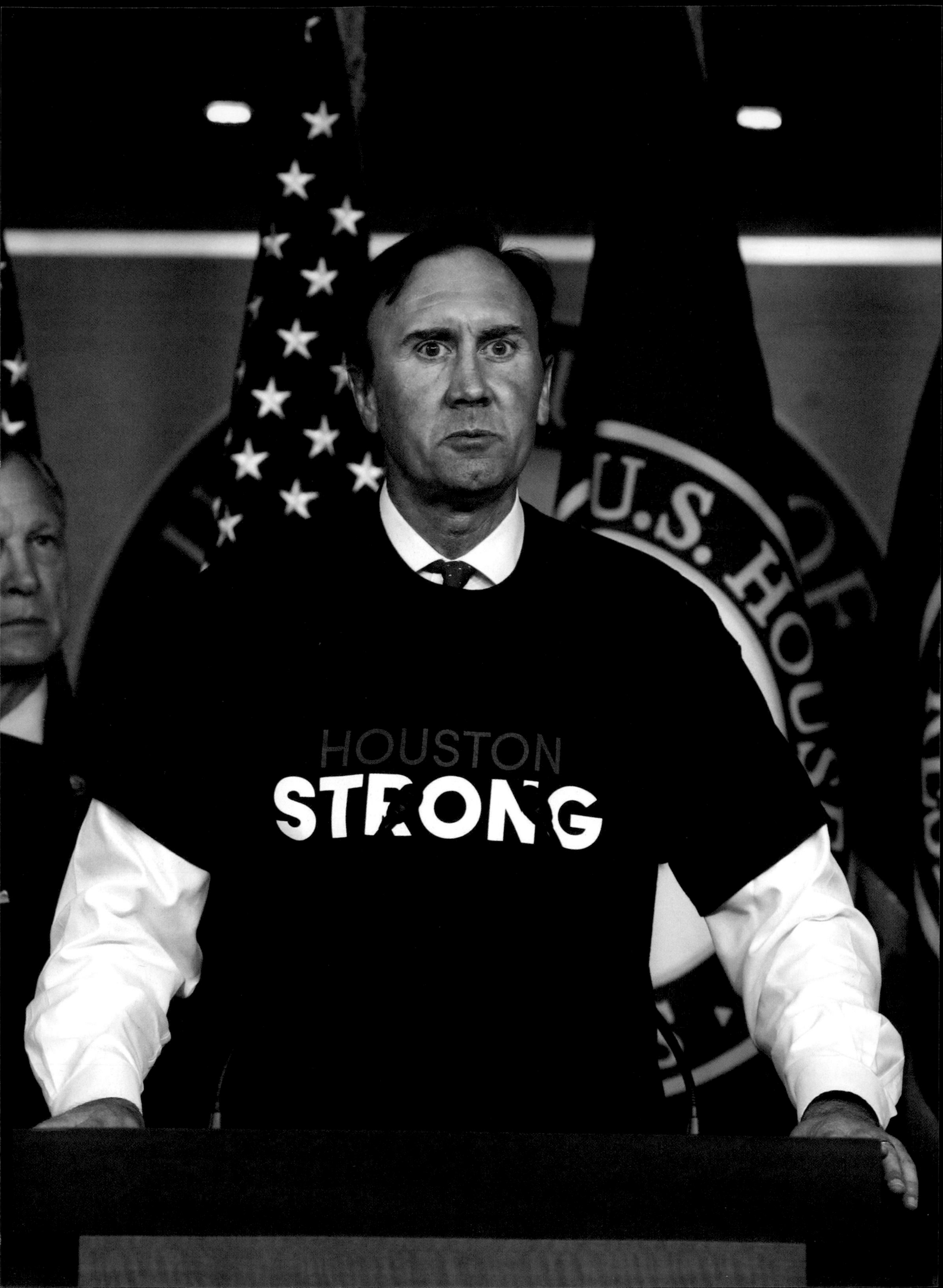
HOUSTON
STRONG

TEXANS IN CONGRESS FACE DAUNTING NEEDS IN HARVEY AFTERMATH

In the coming days, weeks, months – and even years – it will be up to the state's 38-member congressional delegation to imagine and legislate what Southeast Texas' "new normal" will look like after Hurricane Harvey.

By Abby Livingston | August 31, 2017

WASHINGTON – Even before Hurricane Harvey's scale of destruction in Houston was clear, the lead emergency response official in the federal government declared there would be "a new normal" in Texas.

In the coming days, weeks, months — and even years — it will be up to the state's 38-member congressional delegation to imagine and legislate what that new normal looks like.

The scale of the damage is so staggering that most sources in the delegation cannot fathom what the lives of many of their constituents will look like past next week. But what is clear is that the federal government's role in rebuilding the Houston area is only beginning.

"In the coming months, Congress will play two main roles in the recovery process: funding and oversight," said Brent Colburn, a director of FEMA External Affairs during the Obama administration.

"They'll need to approve the funds to rebuild, but we should also expect them to play an active role in making sure that the recovery dollars are spent wisely and efficiently."

For now, the federal government's role is to support local efforts with vehicles and supplies, back-filling expenses like overtime pay for law enforcement and emergency services and offering up the National Guard to rescue Texans.

Rep. Pete Olson, R-Texas speaks about the emergency funding bill for Harvey relief efforts, Wednesday, Sept. 6, 2017, during a news conference on Capitol Hill in Washington. (AP Photo/Jacquelyn Martin)

But as legislators, their work truly begins when they return to Congress Tuesday following a summer recess.

The array of problems Harvey presents to the delegation affect every angle of policy: transportation, energy, housing, education, the environment, tax policy, emergency response and health care. And Texans have senior positions in Washington in all of those issues.

But, sources say, nothing matters more than money. And that means that other than the Senate Majority Whip, U.S. Sen. John Cornyn, the four most important Texans in this crisis will likely turn out to be the members of the House Appropriations Committee: U.S. Reps. Henry Cuellar, D-Laredo, John Carter, R-Round Rock, John Culberson, R-Houston, and Kay Granger, R-Fort Worth.

U.S. Rep. Sheila Jackson Lee, D-Houston, projected the rebuilding process "will take many years."

"Upon returning to Washington, I expect Democrats and Republicans to join together and do what Americans have always in times of extreme crisis: sacrifice self-interests for the greater good to help those reeling from catastrophe reclaim their lives."

A spokeswoman for U.S. Rep. Pete Sessions, R-Dallas, stressed the urgency of the situation.

"Chairman Sessions wants to ensure the people of South Texas have the relief resources they need as soon as possible," Caroline Boothe told the Tribune.

So far, the delegation is working together, and they agree: The most immediate issue is money.

Jackson Lee got out early and asked for an initial round of $152 billion in support from the federal government. Similarly, Sessions asked earlier this week for a "clean" initial funding bill that will not include unrelated issues.

Neither are likely to happen, several Texas GOP congressional sources told the Tribune.

That is because Harvey did not happen in a vacuum. A week ago, members of Congress were already bracing for fights over keeping the government funded past Sept. 30, raising the debit limit and funding a border wall.

In a matter of days, Harvey displaced all of those priorities.

The most likely bet is there will be a short-term funding measure directed to Houston, its outlying areas and the rest of the affected Gulf Coast, according to delegation sources. That legislation will likely be part of one large deal that includes continuing to fund the government and raising the debt ceiling.

Vice President Mike Pence said on a Thursday trip to the region that he anticipated bipartisan support for the funding.

Then, later in the fall, Congress will likely take up a larger bill to address the Harvey aftermath, once members have a better handle on the magnitude of the destruction.

How President Donald Trump will react to this crisis is the largest unknown. In recent weeks, he threatened to shut down the government if Congress does not fund his proposed border wall.

That border wall already had a lukewarm response among the Texas members. But among several Texas staffers interviewed, the border wall is now an even more diminished priority.

A shutdown, however, is a downright chilling concept among Texans right now, as bureaucrats are needed to process FEMA and flood insurance claims for Harvey victims.

"I cannot see a government shutdown," said a GOP delegation source who was not authorized to speak on the record, adding that he did not expect the threat of a shutdown to affect the emergency response.

"Where the government shutdown is really going to shut down are the employees who process [flood insurance] and FEMA grants," he said.

Beyond looking back at past storms as their frames of reference, members and staffers alike in the delegation cannot even begin to imagine what Houston's future will look like. The circumstances are simply too overwhelming in their districts and, in many cases, in their personal lives.

There will be, however, an opportunity amid all of the destruction to re-evaluate how to prevent such destruction in the future and to improve life down the road. For instance, the city of New Orleans used Katrina to improve its decrepit public school system. And amid the destruction of Sandy, New Jersey officials found ways to improve structural architecture and to create more useful and aesthetic sea walls.

"Every time you rebuild you have the opportunity to rebuild stronger," said Colburn, the Obama FEMA official. "But it doesn't just happen, it has to be a conscious decision, and it takes hard and dedicated work from everyone involved." ★

Rockport, Texas USA Aug. 28, 2017: Texas Gov. Greg Abbott (in wheelchair) tours Hurricane Harvey storm damage in Rockport about 30 miles north of Corpus Christi, three days after the historic Category 4 storm made landfall along the Texas Coast. Photo by Bob Daemmrich

FOR LOW-INCOME TEXANS, A TOUGHER ROAD TO RECOVERY

There's no doubt the lives of tens of thousands of Texans have been upended by Hurricane Harvey, but it's low-income Texans who will face a tougher road to recovery.

By Alexa Ura | September 1, 2017

Brandon Olivarez and Tesa Rutherford had barely lived in Rockport for a week before they rushed to abandon their new community.

The couple had just moved into a mobile home in the small beachside town, dreaming of working on a fixer-upper home and a beach wedding in March. But their bliss was abruptly interrupted by the weather forecast, which they watched for a day before accepting it was time to leave.

By the time Hurricane Harvey's violent winds and storm surge ravaged their home last week, Olivarez and Rutherford were settling into two cots they had pushed together at an emergency shelter in North Austin and searching for updates on social media and the news. Rockport, they would find out, faced some of the worst destruction from the storm's initial landfall as a Category 4 hurricane.

On a quick trip back home Sunday, they realized that all they had left was their car, their clothes and a newly rescued German shepherd puppy — discovered near the debris of what's left of their home — who they named Harvey.

"It was kind of an in-the-moment thing at the wrong time," Olivarez, a concrete construction worker but who's out of work for now, said this week from the Austin shelter. You can't lay out concrete while it's wet, Rutherford added with a small smile.

With the flood waters and rivers still swelling in some communities dotting Harvey's devastating path, it's difficult to determine

Tesa Rutherford, 21, and her fiancé Brandon Olivarez, 22, recently moved to Rockport, Texas and lost everything with the damage of Hurricane Harvey. When they went to check on their property, they found a puppy, rescued him and named him Harvey. Photo by Laura Skelding

95

the exact extent of the destruction, which includes damaged homes, impassable roads, downed trees and power outages. There's no doubt the lives of tens of thousands of Texans have been upended.

But as rescue efforts slowly turn to recovery — which is expected to last several years — those assisting with long-term relief expect that the process will be particularly challenging for low-income Texans like Olivarez and Rutherford. While it won't be easy for anyone to bounce back from the unprecedented destruction Harvey caused, the challenge for those with little to no savings will be even more grueling.

"As hard as it is for everyone to deal with this — disasters can be an equalizer — it's just much harder for individuals who had less to work with in the beginning to recover," said Tracy Figueroa, a lawyer and disaster assistance team manager with Texas RioGrande Legal Aid, which is assisting low-income Texans affected by Harvey.

Massive recovery efforts compounded by inequalities

The number of Texans affected by Harvey is massive. As of Thursday morning, 325,000 people had registered with the Federal Emergency Management Agency as disaster victims, and more than 32,000 people had sought refuge in Texas shelters, federal and local officials said this week. The destruction has been so widespread that Gov. Greg Abbott repeatedly expanded his state disaster proclamation — a list that now covers about 42 percent of the state's population.

Those numbers alone would make for massive recovery efforts, but they'll be further compounded by the fact that Harvey was particularly devastating in many areas that were already grappling with racial and socioeconomic inequality and where the share of residents living in poverty surpassed the state average.

"This flood did not discriminate — that's for sure," Anna Babin, president and CEO of United Way of Greater Houston, said of the widespread floodwaters that engulfed vast areas of Houston and its

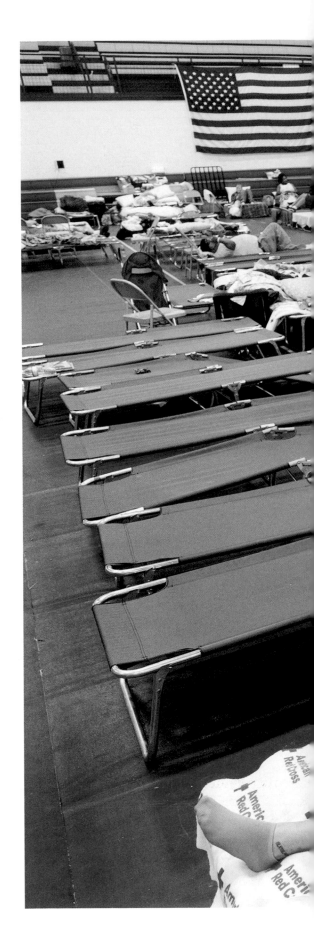

Tesa Rutherford and Brandon Olivarez took shelter at the Delco Center emergency hurricane shelter in Austin, Texas on Tuesday, August 29, 2017. The optimistic couple plans on going back to Rockport to rebuild their lives and their home. Photo by Laura Skelding

surroundings. But it's the low-income Texans who were already in financially vulnerable situations that could face longer recovery timelines.

They may have had savings to cover the costs of flat tires, but they won't have enough savings "to address loss of clothing, household goods and potentially loss of jobs," Babin added.

Others are likely to get behind on rent or house payments and face mounting bills on top of costs related to their displacements. "If they're working paycheck to paycheck, how do you absorb these sudden costs?" said Figueroa, who is working with clients along the Texas coastline.

Looking at previous natural disasters, 80 percent of those affected get to a "new normal" within six months and about 20 percent can wait up to 24 months, said Rene Solis, senior vice president at BakerRipley, a Houston-area nonprofit that will work on long-term relief for Harvey.

But it's hard to tell whether those figures will apply to the Harvey recovery, which will be much bigger in scale, he added.

In Houston, which has seen a high number of affected households, more than a fifth of the population — about 480,500 people — lives below the poverty line. Disaster assistance workers are concerned about the massive loss of vehicles, some of which were submerged for days throughout the city, because they often represent a "lifeline" for folks who need to stay employed.

Others displaced by Harvey could also face dire challenges as they begin to seek housing beyond emergency shelters.

Among them are Natascha Morgan, her two children and her husband, who lived in a dilapidated Houston duplex that suffered extensive water damage.

"There was water coming through the roof and light fixtures," Morgan said from the George R. Brown Convention Center in Houston, which was turned into a shelter for Harvey evacuees. Looking to make repairs, their landlord gave them a week to leave the property, Morgan said, but the family has been spending time at the shelter because there's mold inside what's left of their home.

Disaster assistance workers are still far off from fully assessing the number of displaced residents, but Solis is already worried about affordable housing resources.

Ahead of the storm, almost 60 percent of occupied housing units in Houston were home to renters. But with up to 30 percent of Harris County, home to Houston, underwater at some point during the storm, many existing rental properties that could serve as temporary housing are uninhabitable.

Uncertainty ahead

With their eyes set on long-term relief, disaster relief providers are rushing to get those affected by Harvey through the application process for FEMA disaster assistance, which ranges from unemployment benefits to temporary housing to funding for permanent housing repairs.

At some of the emergency shelters, FEMA representatives are on the ground to help those displaced begin that process. Others have been directed to call into the disaster assistance helpline, but those lines have been jammed, according to Olivarez and Rutherford in Austin. They had tried calling twice, but an automated message said that no representatives were available.

"We don't have very many resources to get a hotel or anything like that," Rutherford said. "While we're rebuilding, we won't have anywhere to go so hopefully FEMA will be able to help us with that."

The couple is eager to get back to Rockport to help with cleanup and start rebuilding their lives. Though it's unclear how they'll find a steady income in the meantime, Olivarez thinks he'll eventually find work again because new buildings and new houses, including the one they'll eventually call home, will need new foundations.

Terri Simmons, Echanda Goodman and Angela Smith sort personal belongings to dry out on the driveway on Monday, Sept. 4, 2017. Photo by Pu Ying Huang

But even short bouts of displacement could ultimately affect the lives of those forced to evacuate their homes because of Harvey, including Juan Mora and his wife, Avelina Mares. A day before the storm, the elderly couple fled Port Lavaca, which had little reported damage but no power.

That's left them in the dark about whether the little income they receive — aside from Mora's modest disability checks — will be gone when they return. Mares is a caregiver at a local nursing home whose residents were evacuated and are unlikely to return if there's no electricity.

Even before the storm, her schedule had already been reduced to part-time work, and the couple was pinching pennies, recently selling off some of their belongings in an effort to cobble together as much money as they could.

"Luckily, we put on a garage sale last week to gather some money," a resigned Mora said in Spanish while sitting outside a shuttered school building in San Antonio whose classrooms have been turned into temporary homes. "We're just uncertain about everything right now." ⭐

Neena Satija and Kiah Collier contributed reporting from Houston.

Volunteer Elizabeth Hill, 8, plays with evacuee Skyler Smith, 7, at a shelter at St. Thomas Presbyterian Church in west Houston as Tropical Storm Harvey continues to affect the area Tuesday, Aug. 29, 2017. (Jay Janner/Austin American-Statesman via AP)

FOOD BANKS BRACE FOR POST-HARVEY NEED

Food banks, pantries and other food access advocates are bracing for increased need in communities that struggled with food insecurity even before Hurricane Harvey – and planning how to meet needs in the months of recovery still ahead.

By Marissa Evans | September 21, 2017

Dan Maher is watching the inconvenience of disaster settling in as Hurricane Harvey victims trickle back into Beaumont.

As residents make their first visits to lost homes and begin the daunting Federal Emergency Management Assistance application process, Maher, executive director of the Southeast Texas Food Bank, is preparing his staff for the coming onslaught of people turning to them for meals. Since the storm, they've given out more than 1.5 million pounds of food.

Right now, the challenge is handling a surge of food donations that have arrived from across the nation — Maher says they're going to need more warehouse space to hold it all. But he knows the food bank will also have to prepare for the eventual slowdown in donations after national attention shifts away from the Texas coast. And he knows the need for food will last much longer.

"After it's all done for immediate responders, their role has kind of concluded," Maher said. "But hunger hasn't left the community when those people start to go home."

Thousands of Texas households impacted by Harvey are now eligible for disaster food assistance, and as the Texas Health and Human

Damon Smith helps unload a truck at the South East Texas Food Bank in Beaumont, Texas Wednesday, September 20, 2017.
Photo by Michael Stravato

Services Commission begins signups, food banks, pantries and other food access advocates are bracing for increased demand in communities that struggled with food insecurity even before the storm.

And they're planning how to meet those needs during the months of recovery still ahead. Before Harvey, Harris County had 669,709 people regularly using food stamps.

People have already started receiving benefits under the federal Disaster Supplemental Nutrition Assistance Program, or D-SNAP, which gives eligible Harvey victims up to two months of benefits to buy groceries.

A four-person household can receive up to $649 toward groceries under the program. Applicants have to live in one of the 39 counties covered by the federal disaster declaration and must show they've lost income, had their home damaged, paid for disaster-related expenses like temporary shelter or home repairs and didn't receive benefits from the federal Supplemental Nutrition Assistance Program, or food stamps, before the storm. They also have to meet income eligibility requirements.

In those 39 counties, 1.1 million people were already using SNAP in August.

Carrie Williams, a spokesperson for the Texas Health and Human Services Commission, said in an email that information about disaster food assistance is spreading quickly and that the agency has been dispatching staff to oversee signups in areas that Harvey struck.

The agency initially required applicants to go back to their home counties to apply for food benefits but reversed that policy. Many flood victims are temporarily living far from their storm-damaged homes.

"We're trying to help people where they are, and we're working fast to roll out D-SNAP sites to help people get the food they need," Williams said. "We're

Damon Smith brings in supplies on a forklift at the South East Texas Food Bank in Beaumont, Texas on Wednesday, September 20, 2017. Photo by Michael Stravato

DEVASTATION, COURAGE, AND RECOVERY IN THE EYE OF THE STORM

Staffers at the food bank are distributing 700,000 pounds of disaster relief food donations a day — more than double their normal daily volume — as well as diapers, bottled water and cleaning supplies.

watching this rollout very closely to see if other changes need to be made."

The application process for D-SNAP, unlike regular food stamps, doesn't count applicants' vehicles as an asset toward their income. The program also doesn't refuse applicants based on citizenship or immigration status and there are no work requirements, said Rachel Cooper, a senior policy analyst for the Center for Public Policy Priorities.

"Not everyone is going to qualify," Cooper said. "We want to make sure that it's as easy as possible for people to get help."

Williams said Health and Human Services Commission staff are pointing rejected D-SNAP applicants to food banks and other state programs for help.

Meanwhile, the Houston Food Bank has seen a surge of flood victims and is looking to the state to take some of the pressure off.

Staffers at the food bank are distributing 700,000 pounds of disaster relief food donations a day — more than double their normal daily volume — as well as diapers, bottled water and cleaning supplies.

That may sound like a lot, but Brian Greene, the president of the food bank, said "it's not

nearly enough." Greene said he and other Harris County-area food banks and pantries are anxious for D-SNAP signups to start because it will mean more people who can go to a grocery store for food instead of coming to food banks.

"We're running right through [the donations]," Greene said. "That flow is slowing down, and the need is not slowing down nearly as fast."

And any relief from D-SNAP will be temporary. Recipients' federal food aid runs out after two months.

"It's going to take more for them to rebound and rebuild and have access to food even when the stores are back, even when they get back to a place where they can cook food," said Ellen Vollinger, legal director for the Food Research and Action Center, a nonprofit organization focused on hunger and nutrition policy.

For now, Maher and the rest of the staff at the Southeast Texas Food Bank are still searching for more space to "receive as much goodwill as being offered." ⭐

Disclosure: The Center for Public Policy Priorities has been a financial supporter of The Texas Tribune.

A delivery of food is unloaded at the South East Texas Food Bank in Beaumont, Texas Wednesday, September 20, 2017. Photo by Michael Stravato

TEXAS GOP PUSHES FOR
FLOOD INFRASTRUCTURE PROJECTS

Lt. Gov. Dan Patrick and other state leaders are eyeing a long-delayed reservoir project experts say would've saved thousands of Houston homes from flooding.

By Kiah Collier | September 11, 2017

In the wake of Hurricane Harvey, Lt. Gov. Dan Patrick is calling for the construction of flood control infrastructure in the Houston area — things he said should have been built "decades and decades ago" — including a coastal barrier to protect the region from deadly storm surge.

"We need more levees. We need more reservoirs. We need a coastal barrier," Patrick said late last week during an interview with Fox News Radio. "These are expensive items and we're working with [U.S. Sens. John] Cornyn and [Ted] Cruz and our congressional delegation to ... get this right. We've had three now major floods in three years — nothing at this level but major floods."

The need is particularly pressing because of the state's rapid population growth, Patrick added, noting that "a lot of that growth is around the Houston area." And he said the billions in federal aid that Texas is poised to receive presents an opportunity for Texas "to really rebuild and do things that, quite frankly,

should have been done decades and decades ago."

A Tea Party darling from Houston, Patrick often is considered the state's most powerful politician.

His spokesman didn't immediately respond to a request for more information, but Patrick's comments in part appear to reference a long-stalled project that experts say could have saved thousands of Houston homes from flooding during Harvey.

For years, the Harris County Flood Control District has looked at constructing some kind of flood control project that would curb the flow of floodwaters from the fast-growing northwest suburbs into two federally-owned reservoirs — Addicks and Barker — that filled to the brim during Harvey and last year's "Tax Day" flood.

An engineer with the flood control district told The Texas Tribune and ProPublica last year that the agency hasn't officially proposed a plan and has no timeline for doing so, in large part because it would cost hundreds of millions of

The Barker Reservoir Dam, which was holding its own despite residents' concerns, on Aug. 29, 2017 in Houston. Photo by Michael Stravato

"We need to look at long-term solutions from an infrastructure standpoint."

dollars. A Houston-area congressman also said in an interview that the Texas Legislature would have to fund it.

Those roadblocks appear to be eroding post-Harvey.

State Sen. Paul Bettencourt said U.S. Rep. Michael McCaul is seeking $320 million to build another reservoir that would take pressure off Addicks and Barker. That's exciting, Bettencourt said, because the Austin Republican "can lift more than the average congressman" as chairman of the House Homeland Security Committee.

McCaul's office didn't immediately respond to a request for comment. But last week during a meeting with officials in Katy, he described such a project as "long-term" and said he has discussed funding with Gov. Greg Abbott, the Federal Emergency Management Agency and the U.S. Army Corps of Engineers, according to a Houston Chronicle report.

"We need to look at long-term solutions from an infrastructure standpoint," he said.

None of it will be covered by the $15 billion short-term relief aid relief package Congress has approved for Texas, and it remains to be seen whether Congress will pay for any flood-control infrastructure projects in Texas.

In the meantime, Abbott is championing a request from the state's water planning agency to the U.S. Environmental Protection Agency to expedite funding it will use to leverage low-interest loans to finance such projects. As it stands now, the Texas Water Development Board has more than half a billion dollars in loan capacity, which it says is enough to cover even a large endeavor.

The need for such a project is one point of agreement between elected officials and the environmental engineers and hydrologists who have criticized them for not imposing stricter development practices in Houston, which they claim has put more Houstonians in harm's way during major rainstorms.

An additional reservoir "is absolutely a critical necessity" if the county wants to avoid another scenario like the Tax Day flood, Rice University scientist Phil Bedient said last year, long before Harvey battered the city.

"They have no choice," he said. "If they don't do that, we're going to get another one of these, you know, maybe not in five years but ... within the next decade."

Harris County Judge Ed Emmett, a Republican, said he'd been recently briefed on the reservoir concept and thinks it's a good idea, but also wonders what kind of development exists in the proposed locations and how that might complicate plans. (The flood control district is considering a variety of locations.)

Congress has generally been reticent to fund large-scale stormwater infrastructure projects in Houston. For years, the flood control district has been chipping away at projects to widen thousands of miles of bayous across the region so they can carry more rainwater into the Gulf of Mexico — an endeavor estimated to cost some $25 billion — but Congress has been unwilling to provide any extra funds to speed up the process.

At both the state and federal level, talk of protecting the Houston area from big storms has in recent years been dominated by the coastal barrier concept Patrick endorsed in last week's interview.

The project, estimated to cost $5.8 billion, would involve installing a series of high seawalls and gates along Galveston Island and Bolivar

Peninsula to protect populous areas like Clear Lake and the Houston Ship Channel from deadly storm surge during a worst-case scenario hurricane. State and local officials have said such a project would have to be funded at the federal level, and some congressional delegation members — namely Cornyn — have begun pushing for that.

But such a barrier wouldn't protect against the immense rain-based flooding the Houston area has seen in recent years.

Post-Harvey, the state's GOP leaders have been put in the awkward position of asking for a handout when they typically snub the idea of federal assistance. But Patrick wasn't shy about that in last week's interview.

When asked about President Trump's deal with Democrats to raise the debt ceiling, a plan tied to Harvey aid, Patrick demurred but also praised the president as a great leader, reminding the host he had been Trump's state campaign chairman.

"My focus right now is on Texans; I won't get into politics," Patrick said. "I don't know what happened behind the scenes."

"But you're getting the money quickly?" the host asked.

"I want the money — we need the money," Patrick replied. ⭐

Patrick Svitek and Neena Satija contributed reporting.

A refinery with heavy flaring during rains from Hurricane Harvey in Houston, August 26, 2017. Photo by Michael Stravato

HOUSTON HOPES CONGRESS IS UP FOR FUNDING IKE DIKE

Houston Mayor Sylvester Turner on Tuesday gave his strongest endorsement to date for constructing a physical coastal barrier to protect the region from deadly storm surge.

By Kiah Collier and Neena Satija | September 12, 2017

HOUSTON — Houston Mayor Sylvester Turner on Tuesday gave his strongest endorsement to date for constructing a physical coastal barrier to protect the region from deadly storm surge during hurricanes.

Though such a barrier system would not have guarded against the unrelenting and unprecedented rain Hurricane Harvey dumped on the area, Turner — one of the region's last leaders to endorse the "coastal spine" concept — said at a Tuesday news conference that he believes it is crucial.

"We cannot talk about rebuilding" from Harvey "if we do not build the coastal spine," he said.

With Harvey — which was downgraded to a tropical storm by the time it reached Houston — "we again dodged the bullet."

Constructing such a system has been a point of discussion since 2008, when Hurricane Ike shifted course at the last minute, narrowly sparing populated communities like Clear Lake and the Houston Ship Channel — home to the nation's largest refining and petrochemical complex — from a massive storm surge. Scientists have modeled worst-case scenario storms that make clear the potential for devastation, which The Texas Tribune and ProPublica detailed extensively in a 2016 investigation. They also have urged local, state and federal elected officials to pursue

Storm damage in Rockport about 30 miles north of Corpus Christi, three days after the historic Category 4 storm made landfall along the Texas Coast. Photo by Bob Daemmrich

113

infrastructure solutions, which they expect the federal government to fund.

Last year those scientists and officials told The Texas Tribune and ProPublica that a catastrophic storm likely would have to hit Houston before they could convince Congress to fund such an endeavor — estimated to cost some $5.8 billion for the Houston area alone and at least $11 billion for the entire six-county coastal region. Such an ambitious public works project has never been built in anticipation of a natural catastrophe.

Turner and other leaders are clearly hoping Harvey fits the bill.

They have suggested that the federal government could provide funding for a storm surge barrier — often referred to as the "Ike Dike," a proposal first offered up by Texas A&M University at Galveston in 2009 — and a variety of other storm protection measures as part of an overall Harvey relief package.

But the $15 billion Congress has approved for Texas so far can't be spent on a coastal barrier; the money can only go toward rehabilitating flooded areas. That means local and state officials will either have to depend on Congress to fund something completely separate — a scenario many are doubtful of — or cobble together other funding.

At both the state and federal level, talk of protecting the Houston area from big storms has in recent years been dominated by the coastal barrier concept.

U.S. Sen. John Cornyn, R-Texas, and Texas Land Commissioner George P. Bush have been leading an effort to secure federal funding for the coastal spine. In April, Bush and several other officials, including Turner, wrote to President Trump urging his support.

But the Ike Dike would only protect coastal areas from catastrophic storm surge; it would do nothing to prevent flooding damage from torrential rain, which is almost entirely responsible for the damage Houstonians suffered from Harvey.

Other flood protection ideas — either underfunded or long-abandoned — have received renewed attention since Harvey.

On Tuesday, Turner joined local officials in expressing support for a long-delayed reservoir project that experts say would've saved thousands of Houston homes from flooding during Harvey, along with three bayou widening projects estimated to cost a combined $130 million.

Turner said the city shouldn't have to choose one over the other as it seeks federal funding.

A flood warning flag in the park along Buffalo Bayou, still inside its banks, near downtown Houston on Saturday, Aug. 26, 2017. Photo by Michael Stravato

"I don't think we need to pick one," he said. "… We know we need another reservoir. We just need to step up and do that — the same thing with the coastal spine."

A spokeswoman for U.S. Rep. Michael McCaul said Tuesday that the Austin Republican "has been working with FEMA, Gov. [Greg] Abbott and local officials to identify options for flood mitigation to protect Houston and the surrounding areas from future flood disasters."

McCaul may hold extra clout as chairman of the House Homeland Security Committee. But Adrian Garcia, a former city councilman and Harris County sheriff, said he's not optimistic Texas will get much funding for these projects from Congress beyond the multi-billion dollar short-term aid package.

"They thought [the Ike Dike] would be the answer to a lot of these problems," Garcia said. "And obviously it is not."

Turner's advocacy for the coastal barrier concept is relatively new.

Early last year, amid the Texas Tribune/ ProPublica investigation, Turner declined an interview request to discuss the need for a barrier. Instead, the city sent statements dismissing the potential impacts — and not indicating whether Turner supported such a project, which dozens of area city councils had enthusiastically endorsed.

"Only a small portion of the city of Houston is in areas at risk for major storm surge," the

The beginning of the seawall on the western edge of Galveston, Feb. 14, 2016. Photo by Michael Stravato

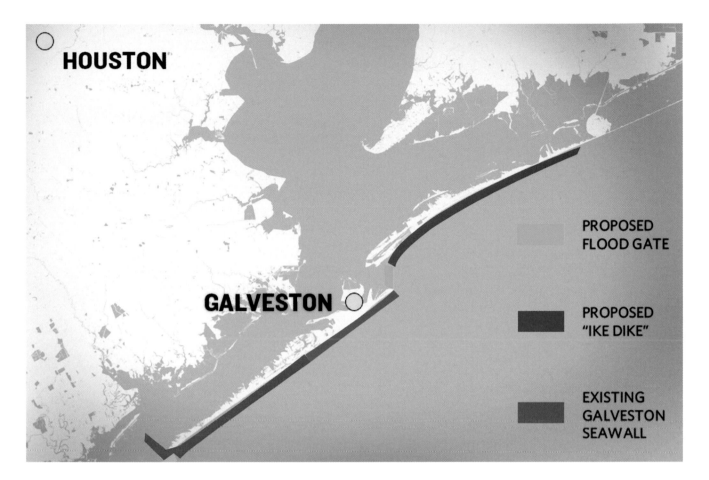

HOUSTON

GALVESTON

PROPOSED
FLOOD GATE

PROPOSED
"IKE DIKE"

EXISTING
GALVESTON
SEAWALL

statement said. "Consequently, hurricane-force wind poses the major threat for the majority of the city."

Reminded of a climate change-driven storm scenario FEMA presented in 2014 — in collaboration with the city — that projected a 34-foot storm surge that put downtown Houston underwater, Turner's office provided a follow-up statement acknowledging that the issue "continues to be a concern." It also placed the onus on the federal government to take the lead on a coastal barrier project.

A few months later, in August 2016, Turner wrote to state leaders studying the coastal barrier concept and said he supported it.

On Tuesday, Turner spoke passionately about the impact Hurricane Ike could have had — and the impact Harvey did have — on the region's industrial complex and the national economy.

"When Hurricane Ike hit in 2008 there were $30 billion in damages," he said. If Ike's direction hadn't changed "we could have lost refineries, jet fuel and the entire Houston Ship Channel, not only destroying the jobs of many Houstonians, but there would have been an impact on the nation as a whole."

During Harvey, Turner said, "the Houston port did close and business was shut down and the country as a whole was impacted."

"That was a tropical storm," he added. "Can you imagine if Hurricane Harvey had come closer, what the devastating effects would be?" ★

Neena Satija reports for both The Texas Tribune and Reveal.

Disclosure: The General Land Office has been a financial supporter of The Texas Tribune.

117

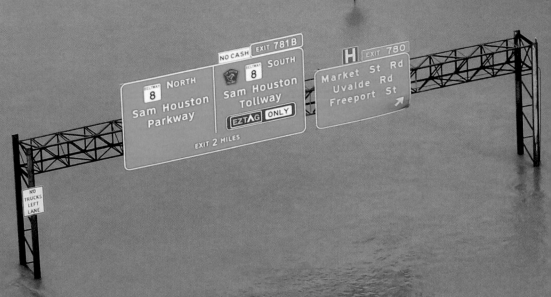

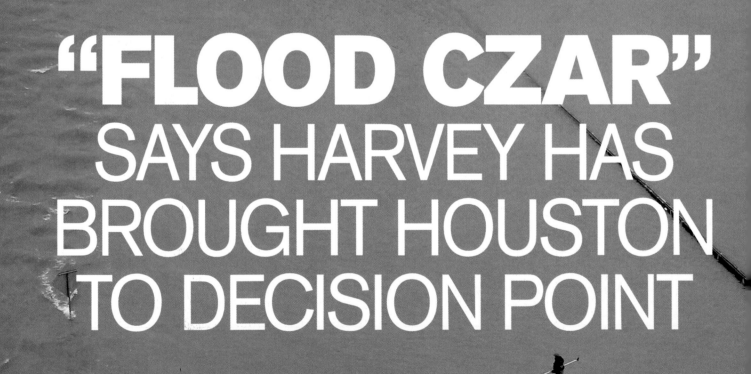

"FLOOD CZAR"
SAYS HARVEY HAS BROUGHT HOUSTON TO DECISION POINT

Stephen Costello, the city's chief resilience officer, expects to play a big role in how Houston spends its Hurricane Harvey recovery dollars.

By Neena Satija and Kiah Collier | Sept. 15, 2017

When we caught up with Houston's newly-appointed "flood czar" last year, he told us he had no money and no staff. That's still largely the case, Stephen Costello told us in an interview on Tuesday at his Houston City Hall office. He now has one paid staff member.

But in the wake of Hurricane Harvey's record floods, the city of Houston is poised to receive billions — maybe even tens of billions — of recovery dollars in the coming years that may cover significant improvements to the city's woefully inadequate drainage system. And Costello said on Tuesday that he expects to play a key role in deciding how that money will be spent.

"Over 60 percent of our infrastructure is beyond its useful life," he said. "So that's what we're dealing with right now."

He said at least some of the money should be used to buy up entire neighborhoods that border bayous and have inadequate flood protection and then to turn those areas into green space. That would be a big change: Harris County has always overseen such buyout

A boat travels along Interstate 10 as floodwaters from Tropical Storm Harvey cover a portion of the highway Tuesday, Aug. 29, 2017, in Houston. (AP Photo/ David J. Phillip)

programs, but they have seen little success amid inadequate funding and opposition from homeowners who don't want to move.

Costello said repeatedly on Tuesday that the city will have to "get creative" to find the extra money to pay for all the flood control upgrades that are needed in a city where, according to Costello, more than half of the homes that have flooded in recent years weren't in a designated flood plain. And he added that development rules will have to change to help prevent more damage from flooding.

Below is an edited and condensed version of our interview.

TT: Last year at a meeting you told residents angry about flooding that 'I don't have any money, I don't have any staff.' Has that changed?

COSTELLO: My former chief of staff when I was a city council member has joined me, back in January. So we've doubled our size [laughs]. So that's a good thing. But we still don't have money. We interface internally with the departments who do have money for flooding and drainage. And we're out seeking additional monies whether it's with federal dollars or state dollars.

TT: So your staff has doubled in the last year from one person to two [including you]. And you don't have any extra money in your department. Will Harvey change your role or the scope of your role?

COSTELLO: Maybe it'll just make my job a little bigger. I think the real issue is that we need more funding. Everything is all about the dollar. I mean, every engineering problem has a solution. And the real question is whether or not the public wants to pay for it.

TT: Last year you said you think they are willing to pay if they come to understand the issue and how much it's going to cost to address it. Has Harvey helped with that?

COSTELLO: I don't know. I'll be candid with you. I think they're beginning to recognize

that there is a risk that there's always a possibility of flooding no matter where you are in the city of Houston, whereas I think people that didn't flood prior to this event have always felt immune from flooding. And I think now they realize that the risk is everywhere.

TT: How has Harvey changed the public conversation around flooding?

COSTELLO: Usually a flooding event is an isolated event. It doesn't impact the majority of the community. And they're usually five or ten years apart. So people forget and they don't really pay much attention to the need for infrastructure investment. The 2015 [the Memorial Day flood], 2016 [the Tax Day Flood] sort of changed that. The frequency of flooding got a little bit more common. And then we have a regional event like Harvey, so now everybody's starting to talk about it. So that's a good thing. It's a good thing that we're starting to talk about it. The real issue is: What are we going to do about it and where do we go moving forward?

TT: Last year you told us that there needs to be a discussion on development regulations in Houston. Has any progress been made on that front?

COSTELLO: We're going to roll out [a task force] in October. And the mayor is really excited about it. It's a group of probably a little over 50 people. There will be a couple of developers, people that are representing some of the trade associations, engineers, landscape architects, bureaucrats like myself, as well as community people. We want a dialogue between all the groups so that the development community can get a better understanding of what the community at large is thinking. And then we can have a frank discussion about these issues and how we want to address it.

TT: Have you been able to secure any extra money for flood prevention as flood czar?

COSTELLO: We created the Stormwater Action Team, going into areas [where] we have known flooding problems and doing whatever maintenance-related type activities that we

The frequency of flooding got a little bit more common. And then we have a regional event like Harvey, so now everybody's starting to talk about it.

have to do. The mayor set aside $10 million [from the city's General Fund] for that. We've about exhausted that money. And so we're in the process of figuring out how we get additional funding. And that was prior to Hurricane Harvey.

TT: How much more money do you need for those maintenance projects?

COSTELLO: We don't know. Because we're doing it on an ongoing basis. It could be in the tens of millions. It could be north of a hundred million dollars.

TT: It sounds like you came into this job and you said 'We need more money.' The county is spending something like $120 million per year on construction and maintenance of flood control projects. How much is the city spending now? How much does it need?

COSTELLO: We're spending over $250 million per year on — we call it 'street and drainage,' so it's a combination of drainage and street and the reason why we combine the two is when you get an extreme event, the water travels down the street as well, so it's part of the drainage system. Several years ago public works had made an estimate that in order to stay ahead of the decaying infrastructure they need about $650 million a year … to spend on their street and drainage program.

TT: What I'm hearing you say is that this is a pretty dire situation.

COSTELLO: I wouldn't say it's a dire situation. I mean, the problem has existed for

a very, very long time. And as a result of this biblical event — [which] is what I call it — it's come to the forefront now. Our job, my job, is to make sure people don't forget. I mean, that's why the mayor created this position, is to remind people that we have to keep continuing to invest in drainage infrastructure. And so the real issue is how big are we going to get? Are we going to be kind of microscopic in terms of doing these piecewise improvements or are we going to go global and figure out area-wide, how do we want to change the way we do drainage and flood control?

TT: Separate and apart from the drainage projects that we've been really focusing on, you have this task force you mentioned and people talking about development regulations. Do you see a component of this recovery potentially resulting in changing those regulations, strengthening them?

COSTELLO: What I see with this event will be looking at areas that are subject to repetitive flooding and figuring out ways to buy them out. I think you're going to see a pretty aggressive buyout program. The city has never been in the buyout business and [Harris County] flood control has been doing predominantly most of the buyout and their budget is less than $3 million for this year for buyouts, which is a fairly nominal amount of money. ⭐

Neena Satija reports for both The Texas Tribune and Reveal.

WHAT LESSONS WILL OFFICIALS LEARN FROM HARVEY?

As Houston begins to recover from Harvey, a growing chorus of voices is calling for big policy changes to reduce flood damage from future disasters. Local officials haven't said much about what they might pursue, but history offers some clues.

By Neena Satija | September 8, 2017

A growing chorus of voices — from scientists to some government officials to members of the public — say big policy changes need to be made in the Houston region after Hurricane Harvey dumped a record amount of rain there and swamped thousands of homes.

With the recovery process just getting started, local officials haven't said much about what those policy changes might be. And in a statement to The Texas Tribune, Houston Mayor Sylvester Turner's spokesman said Harvey would have flooded the "relatively flat city that is crisscrossed by waterways ... regardless of what planning and land usage regulations were in place."

But the Bayou City has been here before. The worst rainstorm to befall an American city in modern history before Harvey was Tropical Storm Allison, which dumped more than 40 inches of rain on Houston in five days, flooding 73,000 residences and 95,000 vehicles. Allison caused $5 billion in damage to Harris County alone — and Harvey's cost is expected to soar well past that level.

Houston and Harris County officials pursued a number of major policy changes after Allison. Some of them had modest success;

Trees rise from a field submerged by water from the flooded Brazos River in the aftermath of Hurricane Harvey Friday, Sept. 1, 2017, near Freeport, Tex. (AP Photo/Charlie Riedel)

The Brazos River crested its banks off of U.S. Highway 59 near Sugarland on Aug. 28, 2017. Photo by Pu Ying Huang.

some were abject failures. Many are likely to come up again after Harvey, on an even bigger scale than before. Here are the big ones:

Buying out homes most likely to flood again

Just months after Allison, Harris County began to pay people to leave their homes, ultimately spending hundreds of millions of dollars of mostly federal money. The county targeted thousands of families who suffered flood damage and lived in 100-year floodplains — areas with at least a 1 percent chance of flooding in a given year. The idea was that it would be cheaper to pay residents to live elsewhere than to constantly pay out flood insurance claims.

Experts say the program was a good one but didn't go far enough. Since Allison, the county's

flood control district has purchased about 2,400 homes, but a recent study said that at least 3,300 more should be targeted for immediate buyouts. Even if those homes were bought out, that still leaves tens of thousands in the 100-year floodplain.

Local officials will surely ask for more money to buy out homes after Harvey. But they'll have to depend largely on the generosity of Congress — and if they get more money, they'll have to convince many Houstonians who haven't been willing to take the money and move after previous floods.

The Harris County Flood Control District has already started asking homeowners whether they're interested in buyouts post-Harvey, though no money is available yet.

"Buyouts are on the table ... voluntary and involuntary," said Harris County Judge Ed Emmett. "That's got to be an option."

Re-mapping the floodplain

Harris County devoted tens of millions of federal dollars after Tropical Storm Allison to re-map its floodplains. The process took a lot longer than expected and resulted in numerous lawsuits. But experts say the redrawn maps still don't reflect the true floodplains.

That's partly because the flood maps don't account for what climate scientists say is an increase in the number and frequency of massive rainfall events. Harris County is in the middle of a large study that could result in updating some of those rainfall expectations.

There may be calls to re-map floodplains again after Harvey. But if Texas officials secure the money to do it, it would take years. Meanwhile, experts also say the whole concept of the 100-year floodplain is becoming less and less useful. During Tropical Storm Allison, more than half the homes that flooded were outside the 100-year floodplain; that didn't change during subsequent floods even after the maps were updated.

Restricting building in flood-prone areas

As part of a broad effort to revisit development policies after the devastation of Tropical Storm Allison, in 2006 the city of Houston tried to restrict building in the "floodway" — an area within the floodplain that is at particular risk of being damaged by flooding because it's directly in the central current of floodwaters.

It seemed like a no-brainer to many at the time. Since the mid-1960s — well before people fully understood what floodplains were — a Houston ordinance had technically forbidden building in a floodway. But the policy was riddled with exceptions that led to thousands of dwellings being built in floodways. Five years after Allison, the city decided to get rid of those exceptions.

The result was a political catastrophe. As the floodplain maps were redrawn after Allison, hundreds of new properties were suddenly included in the floodway. That meant their owners could no longer renovate them or build anything new. Property values dropped instantly. A series of lawsuits and a political firestorm pressured the Houston City Council

Clear Lake has jumped its banks into a parking lot in Clear Lake, Texas on Saturday Aug. 26, 2017, after a day of rain from Hurricane Harvey. Photo by Michael Stravato

into severely weakening the restrictions two years later.

Today, some members of the public and scientists are mystified that it is still possible to build in the floodway in the city of Houston. But many people who strongly opposed the floodway ordinance are still influential in Houston.

For instance, Paul Bettencourt — now a Republican state senator — was tax assessor for Harris County when the floodway ordinance was adopted. At the time he bitterly complained that the policy would cost the area millions in tax revenue. And Adrian Garcia, then a city councilman who would later serve as Harris County sheriff, represented many residents who lived in floodways.

Garcia, now a private consultant, said he doesn't regret weakening the restrictions. "The floodway ordinance was just a fraction of the solution," he said. "If we were to take a truly comprehensive, multi-dimensional approach to our flooding and drainage issues, then it could be brought to the table as part of a total package."

Updating old infrastructure

After Allison, federal disaster relief money helped accelerate projects the county was already working on, such as upgrading the infrastructure around the bayous that carry floodwater through and away from Houston. Hundreds of millions of federal and local dollars have already been spent, and Harvey may help secure more money needed to finish these projects.

But many of the bayou upgrades have taken years longer than anticipated, and the damage from Harvey might set them even farther back. Meanwhile, none of this work would prevent flooding from a massive event like Harvey. Flood control officials say the upgrades wouldn't even protect homes from events on a much

smaller scale than Harvey, like the 2016 Tax Day floods.

Harvey has widely been referred to as at least a 500-year flood — a disaster with just a .2 percent chance of occurring in any given year. Flood control officials say protecting neighborhoods surrounding all of Harris County's bayous from just a 100-year flood would cost $25 billion.

Currently, the county has been spending about $80 million a year on these upgrades. At that rate it would take 400 years to get the job done. Harvey relief dollars may increase that level of spending, but it's still a daunting task.

On top of public works projects around bayous, the region has also tried to improve its dismal drainage system. Former Mayor Annise Parker's "Rebuild Houston" initiative, an $8 billion program approved by Houston voters in 2010, called for a dedicated drainage fee to address the problem. But the fee and the program hav been beset with controversy and lawsuits.

Bettencourt, the Republican state senator, said he led opposition to Rebuild Houston because many of its initial promises were abandoned. He added that much of the money being collected in drainage fees is not actually being used for drainage.

"There's clearly a need to take what happened with Harvey and figure out really how to prevent any mistakes that were made … [and] more importantly, find the lessons learned that people knew in the past," Bettencourt said. "It's just time that we collect everything we've learned, everything that we saw and do the best to implement fixes for future generations of Texans." ⭐

Neena Satija reports for both The Texas Tribune and Reveal.

Kiah Collier contributed reporting.

Floodwaters brought on by Hurricane Harvey slammed sandbags against Terri Simmons' garage so hard that they dented her garage door. Photo by Pu Ying Huang

Carlos Vasquez runs through the rain with his 3-year-old daughter Madeline, who has Down syndrome, on Monday, Aug. 28, 2017. A city truck evacuated them from their flooded neighborhood in north Houston to the downtown convention center, where they will join more than 3000 other evacuees who have fled Harvey's rains. Photo by Michael Stravato.